SEX, LOVE, AND FIDELITY

Sex, Love, and Fidelity

A Study of Contemporary Romantic Relationships

Kassia R. Wosick

CAMBRIA
PRESS

Amherst, New York

Library of Congress Cataloging-in-Publication Data

Wosick, Kassia.
Sex, love, and fidelity : a study of contemporary
romantic relationships / Kassia Wosick.
p. cm.
Includes bibliographical references and index
ISBN 978-1-60497-832-2 (alk. paper)
1. Sex. 2. Sexual ethics. 3. Monogamous relationships.
4. Man-woman relationships. 5. Love. I. Title.

HQ28.W67 2012
306.7—dc23

2012044893

TABLE OF CONTENTS

List of Tables

LIST OF FIGURES

PREFACE

I began teaching a large Sociology of Sexuality undergraduate course in 2002 at the University of California, Irvine. During the lecture on romantic relationships, I introduced multiple-partner relations and the topic of nonmonogamy. Students were visibly uncomfortable—more so than at any other point in the course (even during the pornography lecture). I asked them what was so important about monogamy and why nonmonogamy was so difficult to talk about. Students offered their insights on loving only one person, wanting to feel special, handling problems with infidelity, and differentiating between sex and love. Hooking up with someone was a forgivable offense, but falling in love with another was inexcusable. A pattern emerged as I continued to teach the course to hundreds of students each term. Class after class echoed resistance to multiple-partner relationships, even if they were consensual, and I wondered why such apparently sexually liberated students were so unsettled by nonmonogamy.

I therefore set out to investigate nonmonogamous relationships as part of my doctoral research. I planned to use surveys and semistructured interviews with nonmonogamists (such as swingers and polyamorists) to assess their general relationship patterns and personal narratives. Because gender and sexual orientation are key determinants in rates and experiences with nonmonogamy, I wanted inclusive survey and interview samples. I constructed a brief survey to assess respondents' relationship rules, experiences with cheating, and perceptions of nonmonogamy. The survey also served as a recruitment tool for subsequent in-depth interviews, which were intended to generate rich data on multiple-partner relationships. I hoped to address the very questions my students asked about nonmonogamists: Who are their partners? What are they doing with their partners? How do they construct their relationships? Do concepts like commitment and loyalty matter in a plural-partner context, and are nonmonogamists happy?

During a conversation with my mentor, Francesca Cancian, she questioned my excluding monogamists from the original study design. I emphasized that my overall goal was to investigate *multiple*-partner relationships. She suggested that if I wanted answers about sex, love, loyalty, and partnership(s), perhaps I should also ask monogamists. Francesca's insight compelled me to redesign the study and shift my analytic focus to the intricacies of sex, love, and loyalty in a wider context. I almost missed what has become this study's main finding: that fidelity can (and does) exist between partners regardless of whether they are monogamous or nonmonogamous. Further, what constitutes fidelity ranges from partnership to partnership and is more nuanced, negotiated, and individuated than I had originally anticipated.

This book ultimately chronicles a range of stories and experiences with sex, love, fidelity, and feeling special between partners. My hope is that readers witness both the commonalities and diversity in today's romantic relationships—and perhaps even gain insight into their own intimate lives.

ACKNOWLEDGMENTS

I am indebted to many people and institutions that have contributed throughout the research and development of this book. Francesca Cancian and David John Frank were exemplary mentors at the University of California, Irvine. Francesca's research on love in America and expertise in qualitative methods were influential in this project. She believed in my work and helped me find my voice and keep it. David John Frank also offered invaluable mentorship throughout the research and writing phases of this book. Not only is he a tenacious academic; he also delivers on his mentor-for-life philosophy, time and time again. David forced me to grow as a scholar and fall in love with researching love and sex. Judith K. Treas, Tom Boellstorff, and Belinda Robnett provided insightful comments on gender, sexuality, and intimate relationships throughout the research process. Meg Barker was keenly supportive during several stages of research and writing.

Dozens of students in Southern California took an interest in my research and offered their time, effort, and expertise as research assistants. A fond memory involves our research team's walking down Santa Monica Boulevard in West Hollywood during the annual Los Angeles LGBT pride parade wearing handmade red "Sex Researcher" T-shirts and carrying clipboards with surveys for bystanders to complete. Several also assisted in coding and inputting surveys, as well as with conducting and transcribing interviews, for which they received free meals and coffee, research experience, my eternal gratitude, and independent study course credit. I also thank the thousands of students who enrolled in my Sociology of Sexuality course over several years. Teaching invigorates my soul, illuminates my scholarly imagination, and provides an ideal context for engaging in sex positivity and disseminating sexualities research.

I am especially grateful to the research participants who took the survey and disclosed their relational experiences on paper. Interviewees welcomed me into their homes, gave their time, shared their insights, revealed their relationship struggles, and offered their intimate lives for this project with little to no compensation. I am honored to share their stories in this book.

This research was financially supported at the University of California, Irvine, primarily through the James J. Harvey Dissertation Fellowship, two Social Sciences Regents' Fellowships, and several Department of Sociology Research Grants. The American Institute of Bisexuality (AIB) also provided a Dissertation Research Grant. I am indebted to the late Dr. Fritz Klein, founder of AIB, whose pioneering research and activism on bisexuality sparked my personal and professional interest in sexualities. I had the good fortune to develop a friendship with Dr. Klein, who often drove up from San Diego to speak in my classes. It was an immense honor to share the lecture stage with him, and I carry close his inspirational passion for illuminating the complexities of sexual orientation.

The College of Arts and Sciences at New Mexico State University provided a course-release award that facilitated the preparation of this manuscript. I am grateful to my colleagues at NMSU for their patience, honesty, and support during the writing process. I thank Manal Hamzeh for assistance with the book proposal and Laura Madson for reading the manuscript. William Walker motivated me to complete the manuscript, subsequently question the manuscript in its entirety, and ultimately take pride in producing worthwhile scholarship.

My thanks to Paul Richardson, who facilitated a conversation at a conference that brought the manuscript and me to Cambria Press. I am also grateful to the insightful reviewers of the manuscript.

Finally, I cannot adequately express my gratitude for the support of my family, friends who have become family, and colleagues who are now my friends. I thank especially Beth and Fred Wosick, who believe in me, encourage me, and never judge my scholarly efforts. Beth assisted in transcription, provided editorial advice, and along with Fred gave helpful suggestions throughout the research and writing process. My close friends truly sustained me throughout with their encouragement, love, patience, parties, dinners, conversations, insights, and expectations. I reserve special thanks for Christine Oh, Cade Kawamoto, James Kulackoski, Jay Dee Reyes, Kelly Gott, William Walker, JLC, WM, and Erik Stelter. Several others allowed me personal exposure to their relationship struggles and successes, which became at times a reprieve from as well as a contribution to this research.

SEX, LOVE, AND FIDELITY

CHAPTER 1

OPERATIONALIZING FIDELITY

TOWARD A TYPOLOGY OF IDEOLOGY AND BEHAVIOR

Romantic relationships retain enormous significance in contemporary American culture. A stable, intimate relationship is thought to be an essential component of well-being and happiness (Klinger 1977; Berscheid and Peplau 1983; Budgeon 2008). People spend considerable time and effort searching for romantic partnerships in social situations, friendship circles, and workplace environments, through matchmaking services and even online. The goal, for many, is to find "the one" person who provides the kind of love, companionship, satisfaction, and intimacy that can be sustained for a lifetime. Such relationships are so significant that they are subsequently socially, legally, or religiously sanctioned through formal recognition, such as marriage.

Marriage is customarily regarded as the ultimate pledge of relational commitment and provides a structural catalyst for sexual and emotional exclusivity through its responsibilities, rules, and expectations. Marriage therefore operates as a framework or master template for intimate relationships that relies on forsaking all others in favor of "the one." This is often thought of as *monogamy*, which is central to the master marriage template because it establishes the personal, legal, social, and religious parameters of relational commitment through dyadic exclusivity. Enveloped within the monogamous marriage template is the expectation that both partners will not only commit to one another through exclusivity but also adhere to the ideology of marital union. Vows articulate the key responsibilities of the marital contract: to have and to hold, to love and to cherish, to forsake all others, and to pledge faithfulness for eternity. Whether these rules are presented in a religious or a secular vein, promised in the presence of few or many, or abided by through belief or behavior, they are perhaps the most influential force in relational commitment.

Social changes over the past several decades, however, have affected traditional notions of marriage in terms of cohabitation, divorce, religion, gender, race, and sexual orientation. Although marriage itself may in fact be diversifying, monogamy seems to be more important than ever. Most Americans (95%) state that they want monogamy, regardless of whether it occurs in a matrimonial relationship (Treas and Giesen 2000). Monogamy is therefore not only central to the romantic relational model; it has essentially become the master template. Monogamy is predicated upon forsaking all others for one special person. Therefore, much like that of marriage, the cardinal rule of monogamy is dual exclusivity, which embodies the highest level of relational commitment and devotion through both sexual and emotional involvement with only each other. Monogamy's rules are normalized, routinized, and institutionalized in paradigm and practice; American culture is decidedly mononormative. Inherent in mononormativity is the notion that one should feel special within a romantic relationship and ensure that one's partner feels significant as well.

Whereas the rules of monogamy appear to work successfully for many, for others there is a discrepancy between desiring monogamy and behaving monogamously. Studies report rates of nonconsensual extramarital sex that range from an average of 15% (Davis and Smith 1991) to 25% of men and 10% of women (Laumann et al. 1994). However, some researchers consider such estimates conservative, reporting that 37% of men and 29% of women have engaged in extramarital sexual relationships (Reinisch et al. 1988). Though it is difficult to pinpoint exact rates of such extradyadic behavior, the numbers do suggest that some struggle with the rules of sexual or emotional exclusivity inherent in monogamy. Friendships, workplace environments, social outings, and even Internet chat rooms are potential arenas in which one might not behave monogamously. For example, there is controversy over whether online interaction, such as flirtatious chatting and cybersex, constitutes cheating (Mileham 2007; Millner 2008). Internet dating sites are continuously scanned to prevent "marrieds" from infiltrating the online system by pretending to be single, offering guarantees that the potential life partner one may find is not already partnered for life. Many of today's relationships seem to be suspended in a contradictory web of monogamy as ideology and monogamy as practice.

The master monogamous template continues to be reinforced socially, institutionally, and individually; however, some actively choose to break the rules of monogamy in order to engage in multiple sexual or romantic partnerships. Consensual nonmonogamy takes a variety of forms, including open relationships, swinging, and polyamory. In swinging and open relationships, individuals challenge the master monogamous template by (1) engaging with multiple sexual partners and (2) being consensual and usually overt about such interactions. Polyamory emerged as a distinct form of nonmonogamy, originating with the free love movement that characterized the 1960s and 1970s. Quite literally, *polyamory* means "multiple loves," and it offers an even greater challenge to the master template through a range of multiple sexual, emotional, or affective partnerships (see Sheff 2006). In breaking the cardinal rule of monogamy, nonmonogamists must actively decide how they engage in their relationships rather than relying on mononormative notions of dual exclusivity. The questions arise: If there are rules for monogamy, are there also rules for nonmonogamy? Why are the rules of any relationship (monogamous or nonmonogamous) important, and does it matter whether those rules are socially institutionalized or individually established? Further, is it necessary to believe in the rules or to simply follow them? Do people break the rules, why do they break them, and what happens when rules are broken?

Relationship rules serve as a key indicator of what individuals value and expect in their intimate lives. For example, the rules of marriage emphasize loyalty, exclusivity, and faithfulness between two partners, expectations that are generally operationalized as fidelity. The rules of monogamy are essentially predicated upon the master marriage template; *marriage* and *monogamy* are, for the most part, synonymous. In fact, terms like *monogamy, fidelity, commitment*, and *exclusivity* are often used interchangeably, although their precise definitions vary. Qualities like loyalty and commitment, regardless of how they are labeled, seem to be integral, essential, and paramount within romantic relationships. Indeed, even nonmonogamy has rules that emphasize loyalty, exclusivity, and faithfulness, albeit in varied forms between multiple partners. But how can it be that both monogamous and nonmonogamous relationships have similar rules, especially given that one seems to clearly contradict the other in form and function? Can loyalty and commitment be achieved apart from dual exclusivity? Further, what is so important about fidelity that leads both monogamists and nonmonogamists to strive for, ensure, and protect it through their relationship design, execution, and negotiation?

The focus of this book is an examination of the meaning, significance, and practice of fidelity in contemporary intimate relationships. This exploration hinges on the notion that fidelity, best operationalized as the quality of being loyal or committed, is more varied, complex, and nuanced than its typical assumption of dyadic, dual exclusivity. Monogamists, nonmonogamists, and polyamorists in this research indicate that fidelity exists in all relationship forms. Further, the rules of each relationship type are key in ascertaining not only how and why fidelity matters but also how fidelity operates aside from traditional notions of marriage and dual exclusivity. For the participants in this study, fidelity is the ultimate catalyst for feeling special and making one's partner(s) feel significant. In other words, fidelity (rather than marriage, monogamy, or even exclusivity) may be the defining feature of contemporary romantic relationships.

SITUATING FIDELITY WITHIN CONTEMPORARY ROMANTIC RELATIONSHIPS

Most previous research on fidelity assesses people's behavior and attitudes within marital and heteronormative frameworks, which reinforce cultural ideals of monogamy. This is somewhat understandable, given the history of monogamy, heterosexuality, and marriage in America. Over the past two hundred years, marriage has shifted from an economic construct and a religious necessity to a relational, affective experience. Still, cultural norms, institutions, and social expectations perpetuate the romantic marital union as the epitome of relationship design (Swidler 2001; Previti and Amato 2003; Green 2006). The rules of sexual and emotional fidelity are both implicit and explicit in marriage and ensure the highest level of relational commitment. Although a new dialogue of intimacy in marriage has developed (Mazur 1973; Giddens 1992; Fletcher 2002; Struening 2002; Shumway 2003), there remains significant emphasis on monogamy and dual fidelity (Treas and Giesen 2000; Cherlin 2002).[1]

A variety of evidence supports the claim that whereas relationship structures and styles have in fact diversified in the wake of social and political changes, the master template remains intact. Even cohabitators (Brown 2005) and gays and lesbians (Lever 1994) are allegedly able to reap the rewards that heterosexual marriage promotes. A reframing of the gay and lesbian movement to further same-sex marriage rights is a clear indication that though sexual diversity is a characteristic of a changing culture, there remains a continued emphasis on the master template. For those who are not legally married, monogamy retains value and remains the ideal relationship in form and apparent function. Shumway (2003, 219) alludes to the discourses of romance and intimacy as "cultural components that teach us certain scripts and rules that govern relationships," pointing out that intimacy discourse assumes monogamy as its paradigm: "The monogamous relationship, whether gay or straight, is our culture's dominant form of sexual regulation. In the absence of other ethics, marriage will be seen by most as the only one available" (229).

Previous research on intimate relationships suffers from a variety of limitations. Many of these studies assess relationship behavior and attitudes within a framework of marriage and heterosexuality that reinforces cultural ideals of monogamy through research design and analyses. Unfortunately, such research necessarily situates infidelity, extramarital sex, and alternatives to monogamy in a primarily deviant context. Doing so not only introduces potential biases into the data but also fails to resolve the tension between the monogamy ideal and nonmonogamous (whether covert or consensual) behavior.

For example, an important limitation in research on monogamy and infidelity rests with researchers' assumptions. Most assume that extramarital sex is secretive, thus tempering the way a study is designed, which results are analyzed, and what conclusions can be made about a particular sample (Thompson 1983; Blow and Hartnett 2005a). Consent becomes an important yet commonly overlooked variable because the script of monogamy is based on sexual and emotional fidelity. In addition, research on extramarital sex includes data on those who are married; what about cohabitation, dating, domestic partnerships, and other forms of committed relationships?

Studying intimate relationships in terms that reinforce marriage creates a number of problems. First, these studies shed little or no light on the diverse nature of contemporary relationships. Second, framing nonmonogamous behavior through the use of mononormative language

—such as *extramarital sex, dyadic* (and therefore *extradyadic*) relations, and *cheating*—is problematic. For example, polyamorists characterize their loves and intimacies in the plural, which involves using language and constructs that subvert the vocabulary of coupledom. Third, because most studies rely on mononormative approaches to research design and data analysis, it becomes difficult to recognize the intricacies of sexual and emotional multiple partnerships. Fourth, these studies invoke a framework of deviance that situates extramarital sex, infidelity, and alternatives to monogamy in terms that fail to resolve the tension between the monogamy ideal and nonmonogamous (whether covert or consensual) behavior. In other words, rather than exploring aspects, constructions, and determinants of fidelity, efforts have instead focused on what happens when people violate it.

Some previous studies do recognize what I call a continuum of fidelity. For example, Buunk (1980) proposed that extramarital behavior can range from flirtation to a long-term sexual relationship. Sometimes people approve of nonsexual extradyadic behaviors, such as going to the movies (Weis and Slosnerick 1981). Others distinguish between emotional (affairs) and sexual (cheating) engagement in extramarital relations (Sprey 1972; Atwater 1979; Spanier and Margolis 1983). Thompson (1984) purposely distinguished among three types of extramarital relationships to assess both behaviors and attitudes of extradyadic relations: (1) emotional but not sexual, (2) sexual but not emotional, and (3) emotional and sexual. Although studies like these have effectively acknowledged through methods and data analyses the distinction between sex and emotion in extramarital relations, conceptual biases remain in the literature (Blow and Hartnett 2005b). Researchers presume that sex and love are dichotomous and mutually exclusive, and few underscore the ways distinctions between sex and love pertain to negotiating fidelity in romantic relationships.

Relational Terminologies, Definitions, and Assumptions

Investigating relational concepts like love, sex, monogamy, nonmonogamy, and ultimately fidelity requires a basic understanding of their definitions. Researchers (rather than subjects) have usually operationalized these constructs in their studies; however, this is problematic given mononormativity's pervasiveness in social science research. For example, whereas a range of studies have examined why monogamy exists (Kanazawa and Still 1999), how monogamy fails (Reibstein and Richards 1992; Hafner 1993), and whether monogamy is biologically "natural" (Barash and Lipton 2001), all assume that monogamy is synonymous with sexual fidelity. However, Fisher (1992) disagreed, citing the *Oxford English Dictionary*'s definition of *monogamy* as "the condition, rule or custom of being married to only one person at a time." Fisher suggested that this definition, which incidentally relies on marriage, says nothing about *sexual faithfulness*. But a closer look at the second part of the definition offers the following: "Now, also (in extended use): the practice or principle of remaining faithful to one person during the course of a sexual relationship other than marriage."[2] The second part of this definition introduces temporal augmentation ("now") and a distinction between ideology and behavior ("practice or principle"); moreover, it invokes fidelity ("remaining faithful") in a possibly finite ("course") type of engagement ("sexual relationship") that, though similar to it, does not have to exemplify the exact master template ("relationship other than marriage").

Barash and Lipton suggested that monogamy usually implies mating exclusivity, referring to a "social system in which the reproductive arrangement appears to involve one male and one female" (2001, 9). The key word, argued Barash and Lipton, is *appears*; their data on biological patterns of animals and humans suggest that the social system of monogamy is much more complex than mere mating exclusivity. For example, Cherlin's (1999) definition of monogamy, "having just one sex partner," seems more accessible. The problem with Cherlin's definition, however, lies in how to define *partner* and in what is considered sex.

Relying upon sexual fidelity in order to define monogamy is problematic because sex itself is difficult to define. Sanders and Reinisch (1999) surveyed 599 midwestern college students in order to explore sexual behaviors and attitudes. Their results indicate that the types of behavior that constitute sex are varied; 59% of respondents indicated that oral–genital contact did not constitute "having sex," and 19% of respondents indicated that penile–anal intercourse did not constitute "having sex." However, almost all respondents (81%) agreed that penile–vaginal intercourse was considered sex. Similarly, Risman and Schwartz (2002) found that many teens do not consider oral sex "real" sex, according to data from 1991 and 1997 Youth Risk Behavior Surveys. Further, of those teens who considered themselves virgins, over one-third had masturbated someone else to orgasm.

Many shift the definition of sex in order to engage in sexual behaviors while still retaining their "technical virginity" (Sanders and Reinisch 1999; Risman and Schwartz 2002). American culture clearly continues to emphasize abstinence and virginity among youth; results indicate that teens are responding by becoming sexually active without engaging in "real" sex (Blinn-Pike 1999; Risman and Schwartz 2002). The question, therefore, is whether the same pattern holds for monogamy. If oral sex, mutual masturbation, and anal sex are not considered "real" sex, then individuals can engage in such sexual behaviors while still considering themselves monogamous.

Given that most Americans continue to emphasize monogamy, attitudes toward nonmonogamous behavior are less than supportive. Empirical research on extramarital sex and sexual infidelity has followed the assumption that when such behavior occurs, it is without consent. According to Laumann et al. (1994), about 25% of men and about 10% of women have had extramarital sex, yet the researchers did not indicate whether those individuals were in nonconsensual or explicitly nonmonogamous relationships.

In contrast, Blumstein and Schwartz (1983) differentiated between situations with or without an "understanding" in order to measure nonmonogamous behavior. Their data indicate that roughly 19% of heterosexual men and 14% of heterosexual women have engaged in secretive nonmonogamous behavior, compared to 60% of heterosexual men and 54% of heterosexual women who have engaged in consensual or explicitly nonmonogamous behavior. Further, 43% of gay men have engaged in secretive nonmonogamy, whereas 84% have engaged in explicit nonmonogamy. Only 10% of lesbians have been secretively nonmonogamous, and 25% have been explicitly nonmonogamous. Consent is therefore a key factor in defining nonmonogamy and measuring sexual behavior, as are both sexual orientation and gender.

Consent is also important because it determines whether extradyadic sexual behavior is considered cheating or is explicitly allowed (Reiss et al. 1980). Notably, attitudes suggest that individuals are more likely to tolerate cheating than consensual nonmonogamy (Ramey 1972; Blumstein and Schwartz 1983; Reibstein and Richards 1992). Moreover, giving or receiving consent to engage in sexual activities with other partners is rather difficult to measure and may range from full consent to a sort of semiconsensual "don't ask, don't tell" policy (Reiss et al. 1980). For example, Kinsey et al. (1948, 1953) found that of those men and women having secretive extramarital sex, roughly half thought their partners knew about it.

On the one hand, this book relies on normative definitions of love, sex, cheating, and monogamy to situate fidelity in contemporary relationships. On the other, it attempts to reconceptualize monogamy, in particular, through the experiences of those who adhere to, practice, deconstruct, and subvert it behaviorally and ideologically. Further, fidelity's traditional definition as "sexual faithfulness to a spouse" is less salient than consideration of it either as "the quality of being committed, loyal, or bonded to another person" or as "adherence to promises or duties" in this study.[3] A key finding here is that fidelity, even more than monogamy, is individually tailored to fit the needs of today's intimate relationships. This is especially apparent among those who negotiate multiple partners.

COORDINATING SEX, LOVE, AND FIDELITY WITH MULTIPLE PARTNERS

Most previous research on multiple partners has invoked a framework of deviance, examining, for instance, nonmonogamists' psychological development (O'Neill and O'Neill 1972; Ryalls and Foster 1976) or the counseling implications of nonmonogamy (Peabody 1982; Ziskin and Ziskin 1975; Constantine et al. 1985; Davidson 2002; Charles 2002; Emens 2004). Some studies suggest that nonmonogamists are somehow psychologically "different" (Buunk 1980; Murstein et al. 1985; Kurdek and Schmitt 1986) and experience more marital instability (Gilmartin 1977; Paulson and Paulson 1970; Cole and Spanier 1974; Rubin and Adams 1986) than their monogamous counterparts do. Few have recognized (in either samples or theorizing) those who choose to structure their intimate lives around multiple sexual partners.

Such literature on secretive extramarital interactions inevitably forms a basis for theorizing and assessing consensual nonmonogamy. First, research shows a distinction between emotional and sexual components of intimacy (Thompson 1984). Second, gender remains an important predictor of rates, intentions, and reactions to extradyadic interaction (Atwater 1982). In addition, the stigma of extramarital sex is mitigated by mononormative expectations of sexual fidelity (e.g., those who cheat are deviant; extradyadic behavior stems from dyadic problems or inadequacies). Therefore, nonmonogamists experience social stigma even though they consent to their multiple partners.

Some publications do approach multiple partnerships more objectively. For example, Blumstein and Schwartz's (1983) pioneering investigation of the ways American couples negotiate money, work, and sex looks at both monogamous and nonmonogamous relationships. Drawing on survey and interview data, the researchers found that sex outside a primary relationship occurs in a number of different ways, whether secretive, consensual, as a one-time occurrence, or as part of an ongoing open relationship. Smith and Smith's (1974) *Beyond Monogamy* suggests that individuals have multiple partners for various reasons that include sexual pleasure, emotional intimacy, and love. Pawlicki and Larson (2011) investigated the ways in which gay men negotiate nonexclusive relationship arrangements, finding that some differentiate between recreational sex and intimate sex in order to engage with multiple partners. Barker and Langdridge's (2009) anthology on nonmonogamy, *Understanding Nonmonogamies*, is one of the best texts examining multiple partnerships empirically and theoretically today.

Macklin (1980) identified swinging and open marriage as two main models of consensual nonmonogamy, although both emphasize sexual extradyadic relations. Swinging can be defined variously as married spouses' engaging in recreational sexual behavior with other married couples (Gilmartin 1977), group sex between anonymous couples (Symonds 1970), partner swapping, or participation in group sex (O'Neill and O'Neill 1972). Varni (1972) found that swingers participate in sexual activities with varying degrees of emphasis on sexual pleasure and on love, or emotional involvement. Swingers often refrain from establishing love or emotional bonds with others in order to protect their primary bond; sex is the focus, rather than emotional intimacy. However, although many couples enjoy the sexual variety of swinging (Henshel 1973; Smith and Smith 1970), they also report problems with jealousy, guilt, and stigmatization by nonswingers (Paulson and Paulson 1970; Denfeld 1974). Swinging gained popularity in the 1970s, and many individuals today engage in partner swapping, swinging, or other group sex activities. In fact, Bergstrand and Sinski's (2010) *Swinging in America* suggests that swinging is more popular than ever and may even provide a more realistic blueprint for today's relationships.

Open marriage is characterized by a couple's mutual decision to allow one or both partners to have consensual, independent sexual relationships with outside individuals (Knapp 1976; Macklin 1980). Knapp and Whitehurst (1977) found that couples in open marriages enjoy freedom through such an arrangement, although many also reported problems with jealousy, possessiveness, loneliness, and the continued need to negotiate their relationship. Due to increases in cohabitation, committed nonmarital relationships, domestic partnerships, and same-sex civil unions, I refer to open marriage using the more inclusive phrase *open relationship*.

In both swinging and open relationships, primary partners are concerned with protecting love between them and are often resistant to establishing emotional intimacy with others. Love has been given enormous emphasis in American society, although romantic love is a relatively new concept (Cancian 1987; Fisher 1992; Evans 1993; Cherlin 1999; Wade et al. 2009). Marriage occurred for primarily economic or political reasons until the nineteenth century, when marriage for love became the dominant ideal. Coltrane and Collins (2001) referred to this shift as "the love revolution." Cancian (1987) documented the historical and sociological implications of the industrial revolution and gender on love in America through qualitative research with 133 adults, finding that the definition of love is more multidimensional than merely "romance." Cancian conceptualized love between individuals as expressing affection and positive feelings and providing care for each other. Love includes a commitment to provide care and express affection through difficult times and also to give the loved one priority over others.

Incidentally, Cancian's working definition of love suggests that commitment and specialness are important aspects of a love relationship. Even in nonmonogamy, love signifies commitment and priority over others; swinging and open relationships are constructed to incorporate sex but not love with others. In fact, many nonmonogamists experience jealousy and possessiveness when a primary partner develops intimate feelings or love for an outside partner. Partners often establish limits regarding how much extradyadic emotional intimacy is allowed in order to preserve the love in the primary bond. This is not the case, however, among polyamorists.

Polyamory in Discourse and Practice

Whereas some forms of nonmonogamy focus on multiple sexual partners, polyamory actively emphasizes romantic, love bonds between multiple partners. Some polyamorists invoke a dyadic, primary-partner design, and others eschew the mononormative template for more fluid relational arrangements involving multiple primaries or no primaries (Munson and Stelboum 1999). Polyamorists often fall in love with multiple partners and rarely restrict emotional intimacy with others, although commitment remains part of polyamorous relationships. For example, Cook (2005) interviewed seven long-term polyamorous couples, finding that mutual appreciation, emotional closeness, communication, and flexibility contributed to maintaining commitment in a primary relationship. Therefore, fidelity is also salient within polyamory; however, it is not necessarily dictated by either sexual or emotional exclusivity.

What literature exists on polyamory is largely instructional rather than analytical or sociological (Noel 2006). Books like *The Ethical Slut* (Easton and Liszt 1997) and *The New Love without Limits* (Anapol 1997) act as primers and resource manuals for those who wish to commence or are already engaged in polyamorous relationships. Recent scholarly efforts on polyamory are located within a cultural dialogue that seeks to challenge hegemonic narratives by illustrating the pervasive influences of heteronormativity and mononormativity in theory, practice, and research (Rich 1994; Lehr 1999; Warner 1999; Josephson 2005; Pieper and Bauer 2005). Several interviews with and ethnographies of polyamorists focus primarily on the discourse and politics of poly identities (Overall 1998; Mint 2004a; Strassberg 2003; Barker 2005; Cook 2005), power dynamics in polyamory (Sheff 2005), and the phenomenology of polyamory (Keener 2004). Polyamory has remained on the periphery of research, according to some because it (like other forms of nonmonogamy) "threatens the cultural image of what marriage is supposed to be" (Rubin 2001, 724).

Considerable effort has been made to draw distinctions between polyamory and other types of nonmonogamy (Klesse 2006). Though there is a more obvious separation between secretive extradyadic relations (like cheating) and polyamory, distancing polyamory from other types of consensual nonmonogamy seems a less obvious move. After all, polyamory is a form of nonmonogamy. However, polyamory is often described as advocating an ethically overt, honest approach to engaging with multiple emotional (and often sexual) partners, whereas swinging, for example, is characterized as recreational sex that clearly discourages emotional connections (Cook 2005; Jenks 1998; Shannon and Willis 2010). Thus, a primary distinction once again involves a demarcation between sex and love. Polyamorists actively uphold their ability, capability, and desire to engage with multiple emotional partners instead of simply with recreational or casual sexual partners. However, that polyamorists place such emphasis on multiple emotional partners underscores the value placed on love relations.

Another difference involves an ideology that emphasizes the open, honest, communicative premise of polyamory, as opposed to the "don't ask, don't tell" and "partial disclosure" agreements that sometimes characterize swinging and open relationships. Polyamorists also attempt to consciously resist mononormative language in relationship practice and perception. For example, *jealousy* is replaced with what is called *compersion*, which is essentially taking pleasure at seeing one's partner enjoying him- or herself with another lover (Cook 2005; Ferrer 2008). Other phrases, like *total honesty* and *new relationship energy*, and nondyadic language, such as *triads, truples,* and *quads* are all common within polyamorous circles.

Both polyamorists and nonmonogamists are essentially sexual minorities with subcultural identities that display similar behavioral, ideological, and presentational characteristics (e.g., multiple partners, intentionally structured relationships). In fact, it is difficult for mainstream culture to discern the differences between polyamory and other forms of nonmonogamy. Mint (2004b) used Judith Halberstam's (1998) phrase *border war* to conceptualize this tension, suggesting the ineffectiveness of establishing opposition between already marginalized groups. Mint suggested that this border war hinders polyamorists from being allies with other nonmonogamists and presents difficulties for individuals caught between groups (see also Pallotta-Chiarolli and Lubowitz 2003).

Although there are behavioral and ideological differences between polyamorists and other nonmonogamists, there are also overarching similarities. Compulsory monogamy remains problematic for both groups (Emens 2004; Mint 2004b), and both types of relationships are often structured using agreements, rules, and boundaries (Matik 2002; Ravenscroft 2004). Further, communities are integral in fostering support as well as access to and involvement in polyamory and other forms of nonmonogamy (Sheff 2011). In addition, polyamorists negotiate multiple partners by "maintaining the primary bond" in some capacity, often reserving certain activities and behaviors for certain partners (Cook 2005). Both nonmonogamous and polyamorous interviewees in this study used the concept of feeling special or maintaining the primary bond, a concept that essentially operates as fidelity within their relationships.

Moreover, polyamory—much like swinging and open relationships—functions with some sort of structure (Varni 1972; Ramey 1975; Knapp 1976; Blumstein and Schwartz 1983; Labriola 1999; Munson and Stelboum 1999; Ringer 2001). Individuals make decisions based on consent and usually agree, whether verbally or implicitly, upon some set of rules that indicate the behaviors and level of intimacy that are allowed or restricted with others. Rule structures exemplify the role of disclosure and overt communication styles encouraged especially in polyamory. They also challenge the assumption that nonmonogamy in general is impromptu, unrestricted, secretive, and dishonest. Due in part to such rules, the structure, arrangement, and negotiation of polyamorous relationships have been characterized as political (Jackson and Scott 2004), progressive (Kilbride 1994), and equalizing between individuals (Cloud 1999).

Establishing and Negotiating the Rules of Nonmonogamy

Rules are essential in consensual nonmonogamy, but few have examined how such rules are created and maintained, what they look like, what they govern, how they work, and what happens when they are broken. Blumstein and Schwartz (1983) found that all interviewees in their study used some sort of conditions to regulate types of outside sexual behaviors, protect the emotional connection of the primary partners, or prevent others (such as children or family members) from learning about the couple's extradyadic behavior. Consider the following excerpt from *American Couples*:

> It's an informal understanding, but we have rules. The major one is no secrecy from each other, but making sure that nothing happens in front of the kids ... we also stay away from close straight [conventional] friends of the other. For some reason that bothers both of us ... we try and be discreet and our rules help us keep our private life private.
>
> (Blumstein and Schwartz 1983, 291)

Similarly, other researchers have illustrated the importance of preserving the primary bond for nonmonogamists, as in this observation note from Brecher's study on swingers:

> The sharing couples reassure one another on this score by means of verbal statements and by actively demonstrating in large ways

and small that the marriage still does command their paramount loyalty. Willingness to forgo an attractive swinging opportunity because the spouse or lover is uninterested or opposed is one example of such a demonstration.

(Brecher 1969, 291)

Individuals ultimately rely on rules of some sort to guide and sustain their relationships (Rusbult et al. 2002). Whereas the rules of monogamy are normed through institutions like marriage, the rules of nonmonogamy do not have similar roots in culture and organization. However, nonmonogamists and polyamorists actively establish rules and agreements between partners (Ziskin and Ziskin 1973; McLean 2004; Cook 2005; Keener 2004; Klesse 2005). For example, gay nonmonogamous men establish rules in order to regulate extradyadic relations, ensure safe sex, and minimize jealousy (Blumstein and Schwartz 1983; Harry 1984; Green 2006). McLean's (2004) research on bisexuals shows that ground rules similarly mediate sexual experiences. Regardless of sexual orientation, two of the main reasons for establishing rules and regulations are minimizing jealousy and preserving commitment between partners.

Jealousy is regarded as a mostly negative and complex emotion precipitated by the fear of an intruder's upsetting one's relationship with another person (Pfeiffer and Wong 1989). Although jealousy can occur among family, friends, or even colleagues, jealousy is most often thought of in the context of a romantic relationship. A major cause of jealousy is a partner's real or suspected involvement with another partner (Hendrick 2004, 167). Further, there are differences in the ways women and men react to jealousy and in what makes them jealous (Kuhle et al. 2009). Buss et al. (1992) suggested that women become jealous when they believe a partner has been emotionally unfaithful; men become jealous when they believe a partner has been sexually unfaithful. However, DeStento et al. (2002) challenged this finding by suggesting that the way survey questions are worded will produce data on gendered differences and may not be entirely accurate. Some gender differences do occur with regard to jealousy, though, because women and men are socialized differently in regard to love and sex.

Jealousy can occur in both monogamous and nonmonogamous relationships (Dijkstra et al. 2001). Because sexual fidelity is a rule usually expected in monogamy, the threat of extradyadic sexual relations becomes a main cause of romantic jealousy (Buunk 1982; Hendrick 2004). However, if sexual fidelity is not expected in nonmonogamy, then what are the sources of jealousy for nonmonogamists? Jealousy can occur over any type of sexual or nonsexual activity or behavior, emotional connection, or even the potential for love to develop with someone else. Some nonmonogamists actively resist jealousy as a mononormative construct that denotes ownership and proprietary rights of one individual over another. Others assume that jealousy is an obvious component of balancing multiple partners and therefore establish and negotiate their rules in order to minimize it.

Commitment, which also implies sexual fidelity, is subjective and varies by definition and use (Kanter 1968; Ramey 1975; Quinn 1982). Rosenblatt (1977) defined commitment as a person's declared intention to stay in a relationship. Ramey (1975) used commitment to refer to a relationship involving dialogue, trust, and responsibility. Quinn (1982) found that American interviewees used the term *commitment* in the sense of promise, dedication, and attachment. Based on interviews with eleven married couples, Quinn analyzed how each individual used the term *commitment*, suggesting that most used the word in the context of marriage and sexual fidelity.

There is a growing body of research on how nonmonogamists regard and experience commitment (Blumstein and Schwartz 1983; Munson and Stelboum 1999; Finn and Malson 2008). Some nonmonogamists see commitment as the level of love or dedication they have to their primary partner or to the success of the relationship (Ramey 1975). Establishing rules, therefore, that ensure commitment to the primary partner or the primary relationship are a part of nonmonogamy. Rules that govern commitment in such relationships are rarely explored, in part because of the assumption that commitment entails sexual exclusivity and is utilized by those in marriage or in committed (hence sexually monogamous) situations. This study aligns commitment with fidelity, which can and does, according to the data, occur in a variety of ways for monogamists, nonmonogamists, and polyamorists.

The rules of any type of relationship, whether monogamous or nonmonogamous, are important and therefore exist for a variety of reasons. Rusbult et al. (2002, 15) suggested that because people count on rules to guide their relationships, "the breach of important relational contracts commonly results in indignation and hostile behaviors." When the rules are broken, the result is a feeling of betrayal because there has been some sort of violation of either an implicit or an explicit norm that is relevant to the relationship. In addition, the consequences of rule infractions are as varied as the rules themselves. Most researchers have examined rule violations (cheating, infidelity, affairs) and their consequences in monogamous relationships; few have investigated what happens when nonmonogamists break the rules of their relationship(s). Further, whereas polyamory is described as responsible or ethical nonmonogamy (Anapol 1997; Easton and Lizst 1997), there is debate regarding whether polyamorists engage in secretive, nonconsensual behaviors that violate established rules and norms (Klesse 2005). Reports and accounts of such indiscretions are often concealed in an attempt to distinguish polyamory from other forms of secretive (and even consensual) nonmonogamy. Because polyamorists resist approaching both sexual and emotional exclusivity as necessities, there is an assumption that cheating or infidelity does not or cannot occur. Polyamory therefore serves as a useful lens through which to more adequately explore jealousy, commitment, and especially rules (and rule violations) among multiple partners.

The Importance of Gender and Sexual Orientation

Gender and sexual orientation are key factors in measuring definitions, patterns, and experiences of monogamy and nonmonogamy (Henshel 1973; Gilmartin 1977; Blumstein and Schwartz 1983; Rust 1996; Ringer 2001; Josephs and Shimberg 2010). Further, marriage is a social institution predicated upon heterosexuality and the socio-sexual control of women through monogamy. Whereas marriage as an economic arrangement has shifted to marriage as a romantic, relational, and affective union, such predications are still characteristic of the master template informing relationships today. Words like *romance, intimacy, love, commitment, monogamy, fidelity,* and even *sex*—which are commonly used in academic and everyday life—remain gendered, heterosexist, and mononormative in their meanings and applications.

Gender affects not only how individuals define sex, love, and even intimacy but also what is considered monogamy (Risman and Schwartz 2002). Moreover, because men and women exhibit different sexual behavior patterns (Kinsey et al. 1948, 1953; Blumstein and Schwartz 1983; Laumann et al. 1994) gender may also influence decisions about engaging in monogamy, nonmonogamy, or polyamory.

For example, Gilmartin (1977) and Henshel (1973) found that men tend to introduce their wives to swinging and are usually the first to quit swinging as well. This is due to both the jealousy husbands feel about their wives' having sex with others and to the wives' tendency to enjoy sex with other partners while becoming more sexually aware. Women also have more same-sex sexual experiences than men do in group sex, a fact that furthers the notion that lesbian sex is both stimulating and desired by heterosexual men. Heterosexual men are more nonmonogamous than heterosexual women are, paralleling the cultural attitudes and practices of women toward sexual commitment and of men toward sexual diversity (Josephs and Shimberg 2010). Men are also more likely than women to struggle with the restrictions inherent in monogamy (Schmookler and Bursik 2007).

Sexual scripts are gendered, influencing the ways both men and women perceive, experience, and negotiate their intimacies (DeLamater 1987). Male sexual scripts have traditionally involved more sexual freedom and legitimacy than women's sexual scripts, which have encouraged emotion and love rather than sexual behavior. As a result, women often place importance on relational connections, whereas men favor sexual relations, according to traditional gender scripts. But as women increasingly realize their sexual autonomy and as men embrace less rigid forms of masculinity, contemporary sexual scripts may involve a more contextualized account of men's and women's relationship expectations, experiences, and practices (Weinberg et al. 1983; Hatfield and Rapson 2005).

Men are expected to be the "cheaters" when it comes to violating the script of monogamy, and women are expected to not only desire but also uphold fidelity. Some have characterized this difference in terms of men's cheating through brief encounters and sexual liaisons, whereas women engage in "emotional affairs," which involve feelings (Thompson 1984; Lawson 1988). Further, DeLamater (1987) suggested that women learn that love, sex, and commitment are intertwined, whereas men are taught to take a more recreational approach to sex (Hatfield and Rapson 2005). Men are also more tolerant of extramarital sex than women are, especially when men are engaged in such activity (Margolin 1989; Greeley 1991).

However, as more women today have actualized their sexual agency, entered the workforce, and gained both social and financial autonomy, shifts in the gendered dynamic of monogamy have also occurred. Sexual scripts involve women's upholding monogamy, but women are increasingly engaging in affairs, sexual hookups, and extramarital sex (Blumstein and Schwartz 1983; Thompson 1983; Reinisch et al. 1988). Such data contest the long-assumed notion that cheating (especially sexual) is male terrain; in fact, several studies specifically document the sexual liaisons of married or committed women who relayed their experiences, reasons, and justifications for engaging in extradyadic relations (Atwater 1979, 1982). Further, the double standard of sexual behavior seems to be eroding; women and men are becoming more similar in their willingness to experiment with extramarital sex and are doing so earlier, more often, and with more partners than before (Hatfield and Rapson 2005, 148).

Gender is important in terms of determining rates of monogamy, nonmonogamy, and polyamory. For example, women have tradition-ally wanted monogamy, whereas men have often resisted exclusivity. However, contemporary relationships involve a number of men who want monogamy and behave accordingly, and some women are resisting monogamy both overtly and covertly (Hatfield and Rapson 2005). In terms of nonmonogamy, heterosexual men have remained the primary benefactors in swinging circles, whereas heterosexual women are often restricted in their enjoyment of multiple sexual partners (Varni 1972). The agreements and rules of nonmonogamy have, for many individuals, remained gendered. Further, the rates of men and women engaged in polyamory vary, as do their agreements and rules about multiple part-ners.

Sexual orientation is also central in approaching intimate relation-ships. Because same-sex marriage is not yet federally legal in the United States,[4] many gays, lesbians, and bisexuals have been legally prevented from engaging in the master marriage template. An intentional framing of the gay and lesbian movement to include same-sex marriage rights attempts to change this (Chambers 2001). However, gay men, lesbians, and bisexuals have a complicated history of monogamy that fluctuated throughout the 1960s and 1970s in terms of the gay and lesbian move-ment and the lesbian separatist movement, as well as in response to the AIDS crisis in the 1980s (Peplau and Fingerhut 2007).

Patterns of nonmonogamy vary with sexual orientation. Heterosex-uals are more likely to report engaging in swinging and partner swap-ping, and gay men have the highest rates of sexual nonmonogamy and open-relationship arrangements (Blumstein and Schwartz 1983;

Chambers 2001; Ringer 2001; Adam 2006; Pawlicki and Larson 2011). Considerable literature on gay relational structures, especially vis-à-vis nonmonogamy, has emerged over the past decade (Adam 2006; Bonello and Cross 2009; Ramirez and Brown 2010). However, lesbians exhibit the lowest rates of sexual nonmonogamy and usually favor monogamy (Macklin 1980; Blumstein and Schwartz 1983; Munson and Stelboum 1999; Gotta et al. 2011). Some scholars have suggested that lesbian nonmonogamy is less common because women are socialized to expect some sort of emotional connection with sex; therefore, nonmonogamy and casual sex are difficult to negotiate between women. Further, polyamory as a relationship model or identity is not common within specifically gay and lesbian communities.

Bisexuals have been stereotyped as the most sexually nonmonoga-mous (Weinberg et al. 1994; Rust 1996; Haeberle and Gindorf 1998). There are, however, insufficient data on bisexual nonmonogamy because researchers have categorized bisexuals with gays and lesbians or hetero-sexuals. Some studies show bisexuals in long-term monogamous rela-tionships (Coleman 1985; Rust 1996), and others show bisexuals involved in nonmonogamous relationships (Weinberg et al. 1994). My 2002 qual-itative study of bisexual women found that some choose to engage in nonmonogamy in order to simultaneously fulfill same-sex and other-sex desires. Several also practice *gender monogamy*, which involves restricting extradyadic sexual behavior with a certain gender (Wosick-Correa 2006). Bisexuals, especially bisexual women, do have higher rates of polyamory than do individuals of most other sexual orientations (Rust 1996; Sheff 2005; Klesse 2005; Weitzman 2006). This could be a result both of overlapping marginalized groups and of a tendency for bisexuals to legitimate a need or desire to be involved with both men and women sexually and emotionally. It could also be another way to subvert hetero-normativity in theory and practice.

Ultimately, gender and sexual scripts are inextricable from one another. Further, they continually temper perceptions of and decisions about sex, love, and intimacy between partners. In this study (as with previous research), gender and sexual orientation are the foremost predictors of engagement in and experiences with monogamy, nonmonogamy, and polyamory. They are also essential in examining both how and to what extent fidelity is assumed, negotiated, or violated in such relationships.

THE STUDY

In order to fully assess the importance of fidelity and feeling special in romantic relationships, I administered surveys and conducted in-depth interviews with monogamists, nonmonogamists, and polyamorists throughout the period 2004–2007. The survey questionnaires aimed to quantitatively assess general patterns of monogamy and nonmonogamy, whereas the in-depth interviews qualitatively addressed individuals' experiences and negotiations within their romantic relationships.

I administered a thirty-question survey to respondents throughout California and other parts of the United States. The only requirements for survey participation were that the individual be over the age of eighteen and in a romantic or sexual relationship of some sort. I worked with small teams of advanced undergraduate students to administer surveys on street corners, in public waiting areas, and at coffee shops in the major metropolitan cities and surrounding areas of San Francisco, Los Angeles, Orange County, central California, and San Diego. We focused our efforts on several fairly homogenous geographic areas in order to draw a diverse sample based on sexual orientation. We also attended five different LGBT Pride parades, held in San Francisco, Los Angeles, Orange County, Long Beach, and San Diego. We stood with clipboards and bags of free candy and prophylactics (condoms and dental dams) and asked passersby whether they would like to answer a few questions about relationships. The survey was also posted on an Internet electronic mailing list dedicated to alternative lifestyles in order to gather data on various relationship arrangements (Watters and Biernacki 1989).

The survey included questions on demographics and characteristics of current relationship involvement. Questions addressed the respondents' permissiveness of and engagement in consensual extradyadic activities, definitions of sex, experiences with cheating, and consequences of cheating and nonconsensual extradyadic activities. Separate questions focused specifically on nonmonogamists, addressing issues such as the current number of partners, partnership duration, disclosure, desire to restrict partnership or certain types of sexual activities, and both the benefits and limitations of nonmonogamy.

The survey sample comprises a total of 2,218 individuals who were in a relationship of some sort at the time of the survey. Respondents were asked to self-identify their relationship as monogamous (n = 1,363) or nonmonogamous (n = 855). Respondents who identified as nonmonogamous were then asked to specify which type of nonmonogamy they were engaged in, thus identifying distinct nonmonogamous (n = 512) and polyamorous subsamples (n = 343). Based on subsequent statistical analyses and interview data with nonmonogamists and polyamorists, the demographic data have been divided into separate monogamous, nonmonogamous, and polyamorous categories (tables 1a and 1b).

The monogamous survey sample is composed of 52% women 47% men who were in some type of intimate relationship with a boyfriend (42%), girlfriend (29%), spouse/partner (26%), or other (3%).[5] Respondents ranged between eighteen and sixty-seven years of age, although most were between eighteen and twenty-nine, college-educated, and did not have children. Despite several attempts to diversify the sample, a majority identified as straight (71%), and the rest identified as gay, lesbian, bisexual, or queer. The respondents varied in terms of race or ethnicity; whites (51%) and Asian-American/Pacific Islanders (21%) comprised most of the sample. Data on religion show that most were Christian (50%), although a number reported various or no affiliations.

Table 1a. Survey demographic data by total respondents and relationship type.

	Total	Mono-gamous	Non-monogamous	Poly-amorous
	n=2218	n=1363	n=512	n=343
Gender				
Female	51%	52%	39%	64%
Male	48	47	60	35
Transgender	*	*	1	1
Sexual Orientation				
Straight	61%	71%	49%	38%
Gay/Lesbian	18	20	23	4
Bisexual	19	8	25	54
Queer	*	1	*	1
Other	*	*	3	3
Age				
Between 18-29	54%	64%	48%	26%
Between 30-45	32	28	33	50
Between 46-59	12	7	17	21
Over 60	2	1	2	3
Education				
High School	17%	19%	16%	12%
College	60	61	60	56
Advanced Degree	23	20	24	32
Number of Children				
No children	77%	84%	72%	57%
2 or fewer children	17	12	21	31
3 or more children	6	4	7	12

*Less than 1%

Table 1b. Survey demographic data by total respondents and relationship type.

	Total	Mono-gamous	Non-monogamous	Poly-amorous
	n=2218	n=1363	n=512	n=343
Religious Affiliation				
Christian	41%	50%	35%	11%
Jewish	3	3	3	3
Buddhist	5	6	5	2
Pagan	8	2	7	35
Atheist	5	3	6	8
Other	11	10	13	16
No Affiliation	27	26	31	25
Race/Ethnicity				
White	61%	51%	67%	90%
African-American	6	8	6	1
Hispanic/Latino	11	14	11	1
Asian-American	15	21	9	*
Multiracial/Ethnic	3	2	3	4
Other	3	3	4	3
Marital/Union Status				
Yes	63%	68%	65%	62%
No	34	32	35	39
Time with Primary Partner				
Less than 1 year	30%	31%	36%	13%
1-3 years	28	34	21	20
3-5 years	15	16	13	15
5-10 years	12	10	13	19
More than 10 years	15	9	17	33

*Less than 1%

The nonmonogamous survey sample comprises 49% women and 50% men who were engaged in polyamory (38%) or open relationships (26%), whereas several indicated intimate friendships, "friends with benefits," swinging, or "other"[6] as their main relationship form (figure 1).

Figure 1. Survey respondents' reported types of nonmonogamous relationships.

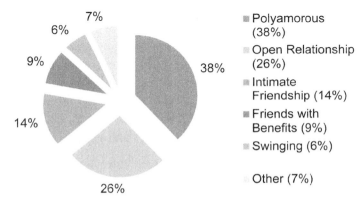

Nonmonogamous respondents ranged between the ages of eighteen and sixty-seven, although most were between eighteen and forty-five (78%), college-educated (75%), and did not have children (66%). Several attempts were made to diversify the sample, and many identified as straight (44%); others identified as bisexual (36%) or gay/lesbian (15%). Most were white (76%) and not affiliated with any religion (29%).

The polyamorous survey sample constitutes 343 respondents, of which 64% were women and 35% were men.[7] All engaged with multiple partners at the time of the survey. Respondents ranged between the ages of eighteen and sixty-seven, although most were between eighteen and forty-five (76%), college-educated (88%), and had children (43%). Because several attempts were made to diversify the entire nonmonogamous sample, most polyamorists identified as bisexual (54%), and others identified as straight (38%), gay/lesbian (4%), or other (3%). The respondents varied in terms of race or ethnicity; white (90%), multiracial (4%), Hispanic/Latino (2%), and African American/black (2%) composed most of the polyamorous sample.[8] Most were Pagan (35%), not religiously affiliated (25%), or Christian (11%).

Though women and men reported similar rates of monogamy (52% and 47%, respectively), there were more nonmonogamous men (60%) than women (39%) and more polyamorous women (64%) than men (35%). This may be because of the prevalence of women in polyamorous circles, whereas men tend to be more involved in swinging and open relationships. In terms of sexual orientation, most heterosexual respondents were monogamous (71%), whereas gay male respondents were more likely to be nonmonogamous (23%), and bisexuals most often identified their relationships as polyamorous (54%). Such results are consistent with previous findings regarding both gender and sexual orientation.

I also conducted semistructured, in-depth interviews with seventy individuals: thirty-five monogamists and thirty-five nonmonogamists. Some interviewees were obtained voluntarily through the survey process, and others were identified through chain referral methods, such as snowball sampling and targeted sampling (Watters and Biernacki 1989; Heckathorn 1997). All names and identifying features have been changed to ensure the interviewees' anonymity. The interviews were an opportunity to further examine the nuances of fidelity and involved a wider range of relationship issues, such as current partnership(s), agreements and their construction, extradyadic activities and consequences, and individual definitions and perceptions of relationship terms and concepts. Interviews were conducted in homes, local coffee shops, and on park or beach benches and lasted between one and four hours. I was often invited to parties, barbeques, family gatherings, sex clubs, formal events, and organizational meetings after the interviews. At times, I used such opportunities to observe the dynamics between interviewees and their partner(s), gain access to additional participants, and engage in researcher–subject reciprocity.

The research design draws on interpretivist constructivism, which is primarily concerned with assessing social members' definitions of a situation (Schwandt 2000). I adhered to several principles of feminist research that complement the qualitative design by focusing on participants' experiences, meanings, and definitions without losing sight of context (Skeggs 2001, 426). Further, my "self" is intimately a part of knowledge production, and my personal characteristics and positionality are factors in data collection and analysis. Ethical feminist research involves a responsibility to equalize power between researcher and subject and to reciprocate knowledge in order to "give back" to the subject (Skeggs 2001). Interviewees were therefore permitted to ask me questions at the end of the interview. I also had a number of conversations, especially with nonmonogamists and polyamorists, about the results of the project in order to locate themselves and their experiences in the data. I used grounded theory to inform data collection and analysis, and the interview transcriptions were analyzed using both open and focused coding on emerging patterns specific to the guiding research questions (Glaser and Strauss 1967; Strauss and Corbin 1998; Charmaz 2001).

The entire interview sample was intentionally divided by five gender and sexual orientation categories: heterosexual women, heterosexual men, bisexual women, bisexual men, and gay men. Though lesbians were excluded from the in-depth interviews due to their traditionally low rates of nonmonogamy, I conducted three follow-up interviews with lesbians regarding their experiences with monogamy and nonmonogamy.

Figure 2. Monogamous in-depth interview participants by pseudonym and age.

MONOGAMOUS MEN		
Heterosexual	*Bisexual*	*Gay*
Barry, 19	Alexander, 19	Christopher, 20
Mike, 19	Houie, 22	Angel, 21
Iain, 21	Erick, 24	Craig, 22
Ronney, 21	Devin, 25	Justin, 28
Nigel, 21	Noah, 31	Brach, 28
Hermes, 32	Marcus, 43	Dennis, 34
Edward, 43	Fred, 62	Geary, 51

MONOGAMOUS WOMEN		
Heterosexual	*Bisexual*	*Lesbian*
Kandy, 19	Jacinda, 20	Shane, 31
Tannah, 20	Wanda, 23	Rena, 38
Brandi, 21	Ariel, 24	Olivia, 23
Grace, 21	Jennifer, 27	
Melina, 23	Natalie, 32	
Marie, 31	Martha, 34	
Beth, 34	Joan, 49	

The sample included mostly white, highly educated interviewees who ranged from eighteen to sixty years of age. Each was in a romantic relationship of some sort at the time of the interview, and several were married or in domestic partnerships.

The monogamous interview sample comprises seven participants from each category, for a total of fourteen women and twenty-one men (figure 2). When gathering research participants, I found that monogamous gay and bisexual men were difficult to locate, as were monogamous bisexual women. This sampling issue speaks to a significant pattern in the rates of monogamy among different sexual orientations.

The nonmonogamous interview sample comprises seven participants from each gender and sexual orientation category for a total of fourteen women and twenty-one men (figure 3). In order to incorporate a range of nonmonogamous relationship styles, I employed target sampling, ensuring that not all participants were, for example, swingers or polyamorous. However, because polyamory emerged as a distinct category in data collection and analysis, I have indicated (in **bold text**) in figure 3 which interviewees self-identified as polyamorous.

Twelve (34%) nonmonogamous individuals characterized their relationships as polyamorous. The polyamorous interview sample is composed of mostly white, highly educated interviewees who range from nineteen to fifty-eight years of age.[9] All were in polyamorous relationships of some sort at the time of their interviews; thus, several had multiple concurrent partners. Many of the bisexual women identified as polyamorous, as did several bisexual men and heterosexual women. Of the nonmonogamous gay men, only one identified as polyamorous. Though gay men exhibit high rates of nonmonogamy, few identified as polyamorous. Polyamorists tend to identify as heterosexual, bisexual, or queer; some actively resist identification.

Researching sexual behavior is difficult in terms of obtaining willing participants and honest responses, and self-selectivity bias is common in sex research (Michaels and Giami 1999; Lever et al. 1992). Further, because gender and sexual orientation are key constructs in this research, using general population sampling techniques is problematic, given that sexual minorities compose less than 10% of the population. I purposely identified participants through gay/lesbian/bisexual locations and events in order to ensure representation of diverse sexual orientations, but such techniques miss a cross-section of the population that does not frequent such establishments or attend such events.

Figure 3. Nonmonogamous in-depth interview participants by pseudonym and age.

NONMONOGAMOUS MEN		
Heterosexual	*Bisexual*	*Gay*
Brandon, 19	Jamison, 23	Enrique, 19
Clay, 19	**Paul, 25**	Phillip, 20
Peter, 23	**William, 33**	**Timothy, 22**
Daniel, 24	Jorge, 39	Roger, 23
Martin, 29	Kevin, 44	Jacob, 37
Oden, 35	Landis, 53	David, 42
Gary, 52	**Wendell, 58**	Alex, 45

NONMONOGAMOUS WOMEN	
Heterosexual	*Bisexual*
Clarice, 21	**Genevieve, 21**
Casey, 22	**Sara, 26**
Marilyn, 27	Abbey, 27
Molly, 29	**Heather, 29**
Melanie, 33	Barbara, 36
Karen, 32	**Margie, 38**
Katie, 32	Georgia, 60

The survey and interview samples are timely and unique, and they represent a much-needed contribution to empirical efforts on intimate relationships. The samples vary with the general American population in terms of demographics; participants may have differing views, experiences, and knowledge about sex and relationships. The samples are also not necessarily representative in terms of education, age, race or ethnicity, and socioeconomic status; however, locating a representative sample was not the goal. Over half the survey sample ranges in age from eighteen to twenty-nine, and another third are between thirty and forty-five; therefore, this may affect the findings in terms of rates of cheating, types of relationship status (monogamous or nonmonogamous), and agreements about extradyadic partners. In addition, my deliberate inclusion of bisexuals, gays, and lesbians in the study may have affected data concerning what is considered sex, types of relationship arrangement, and experiences with cheating. Thirty percent of the respondents had been with their partners less than a year at the time of the survey; another third reported having been with their partners for one to three years. This matters in terms of the types of agreements between partners, as well as in terms of the rates of cheating and subsequent consequences. I purposely included different types of nonmonogamy in the interview sample and provided a range of options for survey respondents to indicate their kind of nonmonogamy. The survey data represent more polyamorists than other types of nonmonogamy, in part because I posted the survey on a polyamory Internet electronic mailing list. Regardless, the data comprise an important contribution to research on sex and intimate relationships, and a mixed-method approach allows for data triangulation.

The in-depth interviews and survey questionnaires are used in the following chapters to explore the range of fidelity in contemporary romantic relationships. Sociologists have only recently engaged in research and theorizing on monogamy and its alternatives; therefore, this research provides distinctive, opportune data on relationship patterns, as well as on how individuals experience and negotiate sex, love, and commitment.

Chapters 2 through 5 explore the categories, identities, and typologies central to this project, demonstrating that there are variations *within* groups of individuals, kinds of relationships, and types of fidelity. Although comparisons *between* such constructs can be illuminating, differences among them are also significant; I employ such terms, labels, definitions, and categories as both heuristic devices and explanations of reality. Initial efforts were geared toward examining degrees of monogamy and nonmonogamy; however, a more complex framework emerged from the data that instead relies on different types of *fidelity*. Therefore, these four chapters approach the significance, nuances, and negotiations of contemporary romantic relationships arranged through a fidelity typology (figure 4).

Figure 4. Fidelity typology based on survey and interview data.

DUAL FIDELITY	VEILED FIDELITY
Strictly Monogamous	***Mostly Monogamous***
▪ **Accept emotional** fidelity ▪ **Accept sexual** fidelity ▪ Behavior **consistent** with Ideology	▪ **Accept emotional** fidelity ▪ **Accept sexual** fidelity ▪ Behavior **contradicts** Ideology

SPECIFIED FIDELITY	AGENTIC FIDELITY
Nonmonogamous	***Polyamorous***
▪ **Resist sexual** fidelity ▪ **Accept emotional** fidelity ▪ Behavior involves creating rules ▪ Emphasis on "specialness"	▪ **Resist sexual** fidelity ▪ **Resist emotional** fidelity ▪ Behavior involves creating rules ▪ Emphasis on "Poly Ideology"

In Chapter 2, I discuss contemporary fidelities that characterize modern romantic partnerships by examining what I term *dual fidelity*. Dual fidelity is practiced by those whom I describe as *strictly monogamous* because they accept sexual and emotional exclusivity in both ideology and practice. Using interview data, I explore why monogamy remains the ideal relationship structure, what monogamy entails, and how the perceptions and experiences of monogamists affect and sustain fidelity in their relationships. Conceptualizations of monogamy involve inferring emotional exclusivity through sexual fidelity and continue to be socially and institutionally ingrained through assessments of monogamy's perceived benefits and limitations. In addition, examining strict monogamists' perceptions and demonstrations of love underscores that dual fidelity is assumed and relied upon through dyadic design to ensure commitment. Strict monogamy is most often passively structured by assuming dual fidelity without explicitly agreeing upon it, a feature of mononormativity. Differences and similarities based on gender and sexual orientation show that the master template continues to nuance fidelity; in this regard, I examine a select few who explicitly choose rather than assume dual fidelity through strict monogamy.

In chapter 3, I expose the tension between ideology and practice involved in contemporary fidelities through an analysis of what I call *veiled fidelity*. This phrase refers to the process of upholding the ideology of strict monogamy but challenging it through mostly covert but sometimes consensual extradyadic behavior. I describe those who engage in veiled fidelity as *mostly monogamous*. Survey and interview data from monogamists show how the definition of sex and what is considered cheating inform the practice of veiled fidelity and ultimately exemplify a separation between sex and love in experiencing intimate relationships.

Chapter 4 explores a central characteristic of contemporary fidelity that involves further differentiating between sex and love for the purposes of commitment; I categorize this as *specified fidelity*. This involves an overt rejection of sexual exclusivity and simultaneous acceptance of emotional exclusivity. Individuals who engage in specified fidelity most often refer to their relationships as nonmonogamous. Survey and interview data on nonmonogamists illustrate that creating rules with partners is a key feature of specified fidelity. Both the nature of such agreements and what the rules govern demonstrate the importance of consent, as well as of emotional rather than sexual exclusivity. Nonmonogamists emphasize feeling special with one's primary dyadic partner in order to ensure the loyalty and commitment once aligned with the master monogamous template. Gender and sexual orientation affect rates of, construction of, and engagement in nonmonogamy, as well as the attempt to preserve emotional exclusivity through specified fidelity.

Chapter 5 highlights ways that some actively resist both sexual and emotional exclusivity while maintaining fidelity between multiple partners. I call this more selective aspect *agentic fidelity* because it requires intimate self-knowledge that coincides with an individual's ability and choice to express her or his needs, desires, and boundaries to a partner. Survey and interview data with *polyamorous* individuals highlight the role of creating and renegotiating rules in agentic fidelity, as well as how intentionally resisting both sexual and emotional exclusivity contributes to an indirect valuation of emotion over sex. Polyamorists engage in agentic fidelity by emphasizing a chosen loyalty through knowing what rules to establish, choosing when and how to follow them, and effectively articulating among partners a renegotiation of the rules if they are broken. The process of rule negotiation is a central component to specialness. Polyamory also invokes a distinct ideology that enables agentic fidelity through emphasis on responsibility, honesty, overt communication, and ethical behavior. However, this ideology is problematic in terms of recognizing the possibility of unethical behavior and rule violation, traditionally described as cheating in monogamous relationships. Further, by referring to rule violations as breaking the rules rather than as cheating, polyamorists consciously subvert mononormativity by not only structuring their intimate lives but also constructing alternative narratives for relationship struggles.

The last chapter argues that the conduit for commitment in today's relationships is not necessarily sexual or emotional exclusivity but rather kinds of fidelity that involve individual agency and a continued emphasis on feeling special. Whereas marriage and even monogamy may no longer be the master template's core, loyalty remains particularly salient. This may be the new benchmark of intimacy: the opportunity to set one's own standards of significance and preserving specialness between partners and for oneself through *personal* fidelity.

Eɴᴅɴᴏᴛᴇs

1. According to the General Social Survey, 92% of respondents reported that extramarital sex was either "always wrong" or "almost always wrong" in 1998, an increase from 84% in 1972 (Cherlin 2002; Green 2006).
2. *OED* Online, s.v. "monogamy," accessed September 10, 2007, http://dictionary.oed.com/cgi/entry/00314586.
3. *OED* Online, s.v. "fidelity," accessed September 10, 2007, http://dictionary.oed.com/cgi/entry/50084378.
4. Civil marriage is governed by state law rather than federal law in the United States. As of December 2012, same-sex marriage is legal in nine states and the District of Columbia.
5. One limitation of this high-density sampling is that gay enclaves such as Castro, West Hollywood, and Hillcrest comprise predominantly middle- to upper-class gay men rather than lesbians or bisexuals. Conversely, obtaining a heterosexual sample using cluster sampling based on geographic location, such as a homogeneous neighborhood, remains problematic, given that heterosexuals live everywhere. The category "other" included intimate friendships, "friends with benefits," and partners who were not yet defined as boyfriend, girlfriend, or partner.
6. "Other" responses include triads, group marriages, multiple primaries, and fuck buddies.
7. One percent identified themselves as transgender.
8. Numerous attempts were made to obtain a racially diverse sample; however, as correlated with education, most polyamorous individuals have been and continue to be white.
9. Polyamorists are fairly homogenous in terms of race (Caucasian), nationality (American), education (college or postgraduate), class (middle or upper), spirituality (Pagan), and sexual orientation (bisexual or heterosexual). It is not common for gay men to identify as polyamorous, even though gay men have the highest rates of nonmonogamy (LaSala 2004).

CHAPTER 2

"HE'S MY ONE AND ONLY"

DUAL FIDELITY AND STRICT MONOGAMY

Researchers predicted a departure from monogamy in favor of new relational forms, but it seems that the monogamy ideal is celebrated today more than ever. Why does monogamy remain the ideal relationship structure? What does it involve, and how do the perceptions and experiences of monogamists sustain fidelity in their relationships? Monogamy has been so culturally and institutionally emphasized that it has conditioned American society's approach to sex, intimacy, and romantic love, reinforcing exclusivity without differentiating whether that refers to either sexual or emotional fidelity (or to both). Though sex and love are often interrelated, they can also be differentiated. A key feature of fidelity, as employed by strict monogamists, is the inferred acknowledgment of duality. Strict monogamists assume that sexual and emotional fidelity are one and the same instead of articulating the different sexual and emotional facets of exclusivity.

This chapter explores those who emphasize strict monogamy in both ideology and behavior using the concept of *dual fidelity*. Monogamists are quick to point out that monogamy means "being" with one person, but they fail to adequately articulate what that constitutes. This is primarily due to the hegemonic template of monogamy; it is not questioned or thought about because there are no socially sanctioned alternatives. Therefore, assessing what monogamy means is useful in ascertaining its benefits and limitations. Further, few strict monogamists hold intentional discussions to determine exclusivity, rules, or the consequences of rule violations. They seldom explicitly agree upon the dual fidelity inherent in monogamy when developing their relationships; for most, it is implied and rarely verbalized. Such assumptions can become problematic when implicit rules are violated, and they aptly illustrate the pervasiveness of mononormativity.

Because strict monogamists believe it is only possible to be in love with one person, emotional fidelity is implied and thus assumed, along with sexual fidelity. Strict monogamists expect dual fidelity to ensure (and demonstrate) commitment, security, loyalty, and "specialness" between partners through sexual and emotional exclusivity. And although the cultural landscape of intimacies has in fact expanded, the master marriage template continues to engender and heterosexualize strict monogamists.

Dual fidelity is the foundation of strictly monogamous relationships. Strict monogamists embrace emotional and sexual dyadic exclusivity in both their ideological narratives and actual behaviors. Interviewees exemplified the particular characteristics of those who are strictly monogamous in terms of conceptualizing monogamy, assessing monogamy's benefits and limitations, the perceptions and demonstrations of love, and finally, passively structuring strictly monogamous relationships by assuming dual fidelity.

WHAT MONOGAMY REALLY MEANS

Although a vast majority of Americans believe monogamy is important, perceptions of what monogamy means vary from person to person. Operationalizing monogamy therefore helps both indicate its benefits

and limitations and assess how monogamists experience feeling significant in their relationships. Notably, few previous studies have taken this
approach in examining the meaning and valuation of monogamy with
monogamous relationships. Schmookler and Bursik's (2007) investigation of how young adults value monogamy is one of the only studies
to date that examines what monogamy means for its practitioners.
Drawing on survey data collected from eighty-seven college students,
Schmookler and Bursik found gendered approaches to the valuation of
sexual and emotional monogamy, as well as to respondents' perceptions
of whether monogamy was relationship-enhancing or a sacrifice. For
example, women valued sexual and emotional monogamy more than
men did, and men were more likely to view monogamy as a sacrifice.
Although their study is a clear contribution to monogamy literature,
Schmookler and Bursik relied on measurements and scales that assume
normative definitions of monogamy in their research design. Nonethe-
less, their findings on the significance of monogamy are mirrored in this
study's interview data.

I asked each interviewee a series of questions about definitions of relational concepts like love, commitment, sex, cheating, and monogamy.
Overall, interviewees were relatively surprised when I asked them to
define monogamy, reacting with side-glances, confused facial expressions, or verbal cues (e.g., "Hmph," "Wow, okay"). Regardless of their
eventual responses when asked to define monogamy, almost all pontifi-
cated with perplexed facial expression, as did nineteen-year-old heterosexual Mike: "[Long pause, furrowed brow, head jolt back] Why would
you ask me to define monogamy? Everyone knows what it means!
You don't even have to ask—'cause everyone knows!" After several
attempts at extracting a concrete definition from Mike had failed, he
finally surmised, "Being with one chick." Many, like Mike, characterized monogamy by focusing on its dyadic structure. When I asked
Nigel, a twenty-one-year-old Filipino student involved in a five-year
relationship with his girlfriend, Jalissa, how he defined monogamy, he
offered this definition: "Monogamy means staying with one person; you

know, 'cause *mono* means 'one.'" Similar was the response of, Grace, a twenty-one-year-old Korean woman dating her boyfriend of two years, Al: "Being monogamous means that you're basically with one person. Monogamy means just two people being together and not involved with anyone else."

Both Nigel and Grace, like others, placed emphasis on the dyadic nature of monogamy, which corresponds to its definition referring to marriage between *two* individuals. However, both Nigel and Grace offered definitions of monogamy that are nonmarital, a significant departure from the master marriage template. Further, such definitions of monogamy are rather vague; for example, what exactly constitutes "with," "being together," or "involved"? After requests for further clarification, interviewees began to explain *being with* or *involved* as having primarily sexual or emotional aspects; few articulated both sexual and emotional exclusivity.

Heterosexuals struggled more than any other interview group with defining monogamy, likely a reflection of mononormativity. In line with normative gender scripts, men were more likely to give sex-based definitions of monogamy, such as "Monogamy is sleeping with one girl." Women, however, were a bit more specific and often invoked relational characterizations of monogamy, such as "Having one boyfriend" or "Being in love with only one person." Gay and bisexual men offered the most sexualized definitions of monogamy, whereas most bisexual women used concurrent sexual and emotional language in their definitions. For example, Craig, a twenty-two-year-old gay man involved in monogamous two-year relationship with Samuel, asserted, "Monogamy means sexual fidelity. If we were having sex with other people, even if it was disclosed, I would not consider us a monogamous couple anymore." Fred, a bisexual sixty-two-year-old schoolteacher who has been with his lover, Geoffry, for almost fifteen years, discussed his perceptions of monogamy:

Well, I guess I've always thought of monogamy as a relationship where you have sex with only each other [laughs]. You know I've never really thought about it? [Long pause] I always knew I needed to be monogamous—but I guess I just assumed what it meant rather than actually thinking about it.

Craig (gay) and Fred (bisexual) offered definitions of monogamy that centered on sexual fidelity, responses representative of other gay and bisexual male interviewees' definitions. This could perhaps be a reflection of gay culture, which involves more sexually nonmonogamous relationships and therefore a need to explicitly state the kind of relationship style currently practiced.

Like Fred, many interviewees assumed their definition of monogamy because they were monogamous. This is a key element of hegemony (Gramsci 1971): practicing monogamy without knowing it or without stating what it involves. There are assumptions within monogamy regarding both what it means and what it includes, as well as about how it operates and is experienced. Again, consider the previously described definitions of monogamy that use terms like *with* and *involved*; for many, this means "sexually with" and "involved in sexual relations." Fidelity is therefore designated as sexual fidelity—the cardinal rule of monogamy perpetuated both culturally and institutionally.

However, several interviewees, like Jennifer, described monogamy in terms that referred primarily to emotion or to love rather than sex. Jennifer, a twenty-seven-year-old bisexual Persian woman, had been dating her boyfriend, Zach, for four years. "Monogamy means that you will not have feelings for anyone else. And that you will just continue to stay in love with that person." Beth, a thirty-four-year-old woman married to her husband, Dan, for eleven years, gave a similar definition of monogamy that included love:

I think of monogamy as being in love with only one person. Like I'm in love with Dan, and although we live together and have kids and a house, I could be living on the other side of the country and still be monogamous with Dan because that's, you know, that's who I love.

Like Jennifer and Beth, a number of monogamous women invoked descriptions of monogamy that were more relational than sexual. Perhaps this is a reflection of gendered scripts or assumptions about the duality of fidelity in strict monogamy. For example, after Beth defined monogamy as "being in love with only one person" in her interview, I asked whether she also considered sexual fidelity part of monogamy. She responded: "Oh, yeah; well, I guess there's that, too [laughs]. I forgot about that!"

Whereas Jennifer and Beth operationalized monogamy through focusing on emotion, Beth's initial omission of sexual fidelity, again, does not signify that monogamy *only* means emotional fidelity. Rather, in attempting to conceptualize monogamy, few interviewees verbalized both emotional and sexual components in their definition; more often, they assumed one through their acknowledgment of the other. This speaks to the dialogue on romantic love and to contemporary sexual practices and attitudes toward sex. Individuals have sex with the person they love, or they love the person with whom they have sex. Articulating both sexual and emotional fidelity seems redundant. However, the phenomenon may have more to do with cultural norms of monogamy and the expectation of and reverence for dual fidelity between two individuals. Brach's response to the question of defining monogamy is a rare exception; Brach, a twenty-eight-year-old white gay man, had been involved in a four-year monogamous domestic partnership with Dennis: "Monogamy is being exclusive to just one person ... giving yourself to one person sexually and emotionally." Brach was one of only a few who clearly articulated that monogamy means both sexual and emotional exclusivity. Although strict monogamy is predicated upon dual sexual and emotional fidelity, again, dual fidelity was rarely initially stated but almost always later clarified through interview probing.

Articulating what monogamy means is important for several reasons. First, monogamous individuals self-identified for this study; therefore, it is important to note what they meant by *monogamous*. If individuals self-identify as monogamous, this implies that they have a clear understanding of what monogamous means, what it entails, and what its "rules" are. Whether monogamists in fact subscribe to and engage in dual fidelity, though, is discussed chapter 3. This chapter is devoted to examining those who do subscribe to and actually practice dual fidelity: the strictly monogamous.

Some described monogamy using a vocabulary specific to their sexual orientation or personal approach to relationships. Several bisexual women and some gay and bisexual men talked about "traditional" monogamy, "gender" monogamy, "responsible" monogamy, "chosen" monogamy, and "forced" monogamy in responding to definitional questions. Once more, this illustrates the importance of sexual orientation as a factor in exploring the meaning of monogamy. Gay, lesbian, and bisexual efforts to obtain equal same-sex marriage rights in the United States involve a framing of the movement that invokes the master marriage template. Monogamy is central to this and could or may influence how gay men and some bisexuals approached such definitions and situated their intimacies.

How people define monogamy may also provide a context for exploring why people engage (or choose to engage) in strict monogamy. With current rates of nonconsensual extradyadic behavior, the alternative relationship structures readily available, and more women having gained sexual and social autonomy, why are individuals strictly monogamous?

MEANINGFUL MONOGAMY: ASSESSING MONOGAMY'S BENEFITS AND LIMITATIONS

Though many interviewees struggled with conceptualizing monogamy, most were able to articulate the benefits (and limitations) of engaging in strict monogamy. Most stated that monogamy involved knowing that one's partner would always be there or available and that it provided security and stability between partners. Many also conveyed benefits like sexual safety in terms of not having to worry about sexually transmitted infections and diseases contracted from outside partners. Several also referred to the social acceptance afforded monogamists, which remained a benefit for especially heterosexuals and also some gay men.

Interviewees described the ways monogamy provides security, dependability, and commitment between partners. This is, perhaps, at the heart of why monogamy remains so important to its practitioners. Monogamy, at least in theory, is dyadically designed to connect two individuals in a unique, special, significant way. This has been traditionally accomplished through marriage. The resulting bond is therefore a main source of happiness and fulfillment. Consider the following interviewee responses:

> In a monogamous relationship, you are committed to provide and care for the person that you have chosen to be with wholeheartedly. And in return, they care for you. You can depend on each other for everything and it's okay because you love each other.
> —Edward, 43, heterosexual

> To me, monogamy is like a security blanket for our relationship. Like when the going gets rough, he'll [husband] still try to work things out, because we're in this together, you know? I can count on him. We can fight and it'll be okay because we still have to fall asleep with each other [laughs]. But sometimes he sleeps on the porch if I'm really, you know, really ticked off. [laughs]. But we usually make up in the morning.
> —Wanda, 23, bisexual

I like monogamy because I know my girlfriend is into *me*.
—Iain, 21, heterosexual

I want to be the number one in someone's life. Otherwise, I wouldn't feel as special. So, if I'm with a guy, I want him to be the only one he's thinking about and has feelings for. So, like, I guess that's why I like monogamy. Because I'm number one and he's number one.
—Tannah, 20, heterosexual

In these accounts, dual fidelity is ultimately the extension of this special, significant bond, providing security and reassurance that one's partner is the one and only sexual and romantic partner. And to strict monogamists, because monogamy is synonymous with fidelity, dual fidelity is both inferred and expected through a dyadic intimate relationship.

In addition to the benefit of feeling emotionally secure and dyadically committed, interviewees described strict monogamy as assurance against sexually transmitted infections and diseases, because of sexual exclusivity. For example, I asked Craig, a twenty-two-year-old gay man involved with his boyfriend of two years, whether he and his partner both wanted monogamy:

> **Craig:** We both wanted it, definitely. It was kind of reassurance. We didn't want to explore anything that would put our health in danger, you know? We had found a good thing, and there was no reason to venture out. We both knew what our risks were as homosexuals—that we could engage in sex at the snap of a finger. At the same time, the risk of being involved with that type of behavior is that you have disease and emotional turmoil ... And for us, it was just that we have found someone [with whom] we can share not only a sexual relationship that is monogamous but also an emotional relationship.
> **Interviewer:** What are some things you like about monogamy?

> **Craig:** I like the fact that I don't have to worry if I have a rash [laughs]. I don't have to worry about it being an STD. In a time where sex is deadly, it is very nice to know to have one companion and that jealousy and all the other feelings that come with nonmonogamy are just not a part of our relationship, in the sexual realm.

Craig, like others, cited avoiding jealousy as a reason to be monogamous. However, Craig and others also described a number of experiences with jealousy in their strictly monogamous relationships, an apparent contradiction. Jealousy has customarily been a concern for nonmonogamous relationships because one needs to negotiate multiple partners. However, many monogamists described experiences with jealousy as a manifestation of the threat to dual fidelity. This either speaks to the precariousness of dyadic exclusivity in a contemporary context of diverse intimate relationships or underscores individual insecurities about fidelity and trust.

Finally, several described ways in which monogamy is beneficial because it is perceived as the "normal" way to do relationships. This is in contrast to monogamy's meeting one's individual needs for sexual and emotional exclusivity. Social acceptance of one's intimate relationship is important on several fronts. Joan, for example, a bisexual woman married to her husband for almost twenty years, disclosed that some of her friends and "bisexual soul sisters" have struggled with strict monogamy over the years; however, throughout her marriage, she has always been (and continues to be) strictly monogamous. I asked Joan what she liked about monogamy:

> Monogamy has this privilege of not having to explain yourself. I like the fact that what people see is a specialness and uniqueness between us since we are a couple. I guess I just take it for granted, but at least we don't have to explain ourselves because everyone knows what monogamy means. You just accept it, and people accept you.

Joan's comment about taking monogamy for granted and not having to explain her relationship speaks to the normalcy of monogamy, introducing another important point. In attempting to define monogamy, many interviewees reified their involvement in a culturally normalized and institutionally supported relationship structure. The convention of monogamy itself provides reassurance, comfort, and commitment between individuals and encourages devotion and loyalty through dual fidelity. Monogamy provides couples with a template for engaging in intimacy and encourages sharing with each other the highlights and doldrums of everyday existence. Monogamy also provides the context for smooth social interaction. People know what to expect; their vocabularies (husband/wife, boyfriend/girlfriend, boyfriend/boyfriend, spouse/spouse, other half), dyadic references ("Did you invite the Smiths?"), and perceptions of romantic involvement are rooted in mononormative culture.

Because same-sex marriage is at the forefront of cultural and political controversy, public and legal legitimacy of romantic relationships retains particular significance for gays, lesbians, and bisexuals. At the same time, monogamy has become a charged issue within these communities, especially among gay men and bisexual men and women. Given that gay men have higher rates of nonmonogamy, those who want or choose to be monogamous sometimes feel marginalized. The issue of monogamy among gay men generated a quite heated response from Angel, a twenty-one-year-old gay man who had only recently begun dating Jared, his boyfriend of a few weeks:

> I don't know what the deal is—I just can't find another boy who wants to be monogamous. Even Jared has started on this shit. He says he wants to be monogamous, but he's never been in a monogamous relationship before. So, like, he's always been about chatting online and hooking up, sharing boys and jerking off together and group sex and stuff. But he swears it will be different with me. [Lights a cigarette and throws the lighter down on the table.] I don't want to share. I don't want to be shared. I want someone

who is going to be mine and mine only, and not wanna fuck the cute boy at the other end of the bar, you know? God, it just pisses me off so much because it's like all gays just want to share boys and fuck around. [Pauses, takes a drag from his cigarette.] What about commitment? What about being in love? What about finding your soul mate, you know? We can have that, too. It's not just the heteros that get that. Gay men are not just a bunch of whores who can't keep their dicks zipped up, you know? Well, some of them are [laughs a bit]. But, like, we can be monogamous, too. [Points markedly to himself.] I'm monogamous; that's just how I am. Fuck what they do. Whatever. [Takes another drag from his cigarette]. Whatever. Next question!

Angel's comments exemplify how difficult it is for him to resist the expectations of nonmonogamy among gay men; the "normal" way, for Angel, is monogamy. Yet Angel finds himself in a social context in which nonmonogamy is common. Angel's remarks also illustrate both the heteronormativity of monogamy ("it's not *just the heteros* that get that"; "we can be monogamous, *too*") and the feeling of being marginalized within a gay community that involves a number of nonmonogamous relationships ("*all gays* want to share boys"; "fuck what *they* do"). Indeed, *all* gay male interviewees at one point or another discussed the prevalence of nonmonogamy in their own social circles, as well as in the greater gay community. However, several gay and bisexual men and bisexual women also related that they enjoyed being monogamous, referring again to the stability, assurance, devotion, and protection against sexually transmitted diseases and infections that monogamy often provides between partners.

During a supplemental interview, Shane, a thirty-one-year old lesbian, discussed the importance of being monogamous with her forty-two-year old girlfriend, Dawn:

My parents got divorced when I was eleven years old ... my dad cheated on my mom. It literally crushed her and I just could never do that to Dawn. Never. I mean I take my relationships seriously.

I'm completely, totally, 100% monogamous. If I'm gonna be with someone, I'm gonna love *her*. I'm gonna have sex with only *her*. Why would I give all of myself to Dawn and then take it back to give to someone else? It's not fair to her.

Given that lesbians have traditionally reported high rates of monogamy, I later asked Shane to share her perceptions of monogamy among lesbians:

Oh god! Where do I start? We're totally into monogamy [laughs] ... C'mon, we're a bunch of women! No, seriously, though, we're pretty jealous and territorial. You know that U-Haul joke? [What do lesbians do on the second date? Rent a U-Haul and move in together.] Well, it's pretty much true. I knew Dawn for, I think it was, like, two weeks, and we were pretty much married. I'm not sure why that is, to be honest with you. I know a lot of my friends want relationships, so once they get them, they don't want to let them go. It's hard because it's always the same five single ladies at the bar. You can go through your options pretty fast [laughs]. Besides, it feels good to be monogamous with someone. You don't have to worry about dating or trying to meet someone at the bar; you can do couple things, and everyone knows you're together. There's something really powerful about that, especially in the gay community.

Shane's adherence to strict monogamy highlights the importance of dyadic exclusivity and underscores that violating it "takes away" from one partner in favor of another. Her perceptions of lesbian monogamy were echoed by two additional lesbian interviewees, Rena and Olivia:

When it comes to lesbians, there's a lot of drama and jealousy. Once you hook up with each other it's like, okay, we've had sex, now we're together. Forever [laughs]. The whole U-Haul thing is totally true. Women are women, especially if they're lesbian. You know, I actually have a tendency to mess around with bi girls.

They're usually married or have boyfriends, so they're less drama and easier to have a casual, friends-with-benefits thing [with].

—Rena, 38, lesbian

I've always been a monogamous person. Even in high school, I dated this girl and I was like, "We're gonna get married and be together forever." I think we were together for, like, five months, but still! I think lesbians are just meant to be more monogamous. My gay friends are always hooking up with other guys, you know, at the club or online; they're always fucking each other. But we —I mean, lesbians—are not so much like that. I mean, yeah, we sometimes get down with other girls, but honestly, there's too much drama. Haven't you ever seen a fight go down at Here [bar in West Hollywood]?

—Olivia, 23, lesbian

All three lesbian interviewees mentioned that it was quite difficult to meet new partners given limited social circles, that women were "more naturally" inclined to be monogamous (therefore, two women together were "extra" faithful), and that jealousy between two women was especially understandable. However, Shane was the only lesbian interviewee who practiced strict monogamy with her partner; Olivia and Rena both disclosed that they had engaged in experiences with multiple partners while in their monogamous relationships.

I asked all interviewees about the limitations of monogamy. Whereas some suggested that they saw no real limitations, others commented that monogamy was restrictive and limiting. A number of heterosexual men scoffed through responses like, "Well, I can't have sex with another girl," whereas some heterosexual women made comments such as "I kind of want to know what else is out there ... but my boyfriend would never let me do that." The main limitations of monogamy seemed to involve restricting sexual possibilities and controlling individual agency. This was especially true for bisexual women and men. For example, Natalie, a thirty-two-year-old bisexual woman, had been involved with her boyfriend, Erwin, for five years. Although she had had several female and male partners, Natalie had remained monogamous with Erwin; she maintained that this was her choice but that it was at the same time limiting:

> My relationship with Erwin is just so good. And I haven't really felt like being with a woman for quite a while. But sometimes, I just miss the way they feel; the way they smell. Like I'll have fantasies while we're having sex about other women. I feel guilty about it, you know, 'cause I feel like I'm betraying him or something. Since we have, like, an understanding about being monogamous, I don't want to change it. Things are really good between us and I feel satisfied. But sometimes I think if we were open then I could have a lover or something. You know? Like, be with a woman again.

Like Natalie, other bisexual women expressed that although strict monogamy was their choice, they often felt restricted in terms of not being able to fulfill their same-sex sexual or emotional desires because almost all were involved with heterosexual men. In addition to this feeling of being behaviorally restricted, a unique finding surfaced among bisexual women. Several mentioned that monogamy affected the visibility of their sexual orientation. Wanda's comment about her experience with being married and bisexual exemplified what a number of bisexual women and one man also stated during their interviews:

> I love my husband so much, and we're, I mean, we're totally monogamous. But I'm also bi. So it is really frustrating because, you know, people assume that I'm hetero. And I'm not. And I fought for so long to be accepted for being bisexual, and here I am, with a ring on my finger, and no one knows. It's like I just feel invisible because I'm married to a man.

Bisexual women and men have historically struggled to retain a dual sexual identity in a dichotomous, monosexual culture (Klein 1978; Dixon 1985; Ault 1996; Rust 2000). The institution of marriage further complicates this, as does the dyadic structure of monogamy. However, feeling invisible as a limitation of monogamy was more salient for bisexual women than for bisexual men. This may be related to the issue of controlling women's sexuality—that is, their personal autonomy, as well as their various self-identities (including sexual orientation)—because marriage has been and continues to be a gendered institution. Further, bisexual men are less visible in a more heavily enforced gay/straight binary. Bisexual men are involved in gay (rather than specifically bisexual) male circles, online communities, and social contexts and therefore find it difficult to retain a bisexual identity regardless of their relationship status. Several did express feeling limited and unable to explore their same-sex sexual or emotional desires through strict monogamy.

Although it is often assumed that bisexuals have multiple sexual partners of both genders, several in this study were perfectly content with strict monogamy. Some chose to be strictly monogamous at that point in the relationship, suggesting that they might later choose to have outside partners if they come to feel differently. Others practiced strict monogamy with their partners and had no intention of changing it.

In addition to feeling restricted, some commented that being monogamous was sometimes boring because they had previously experienced sexual excitement and multiple sexual partners through nonmonogamy. Having the same sexual partner, even if the sex was "good," became a source of boredom because they were used to experiencing multiple sexual and, at times, emotional interactions. While describing previous nonmonogamous histories, several recounted fond memories of sexual liaisons and lovers who had "kept their interest." However, to these interviewees, the benefits of monogamy in their particular relationships outweighed the limitation of boredom.

Finally, two interviewees conveyed frustration with strict monogamy, suggesting problems with the philosophical notion that all one's emotional and sexual needs can (or should) be met by one person. Houie, a twenty-two-year-old bisexual man currently dating a bisexual woman, Lyla, had always been strictly monogamous in his relationships with both men and women. When I asked him what the limitations of monogamy were, he replied:

> Lately, I've been pondering this whole thing about whether one person can meet all your needs. I just think it's a big responsibility to put on someone's shoulders, you know? Like, it's not because I'm bi, but more that I just love Lyla so much that I almost don't want to make her have that responsibility of meeting my sexual, emotional, spiritual, and mental needs. Don't get me wrong ... she's the best thing that ever happened to me. But I just ... I just [pauses to think] ... I just wonder if monogamy makes people work harder than they need to work in relationships.

Even though Houie expressed concern about Lyla's having to "work hard" to meet his needs, he maintained that he preferred to be strictly monogamous in his relationship. And as they did for most other interviewees, for Houie the benefits outweighed the limitations of monogamy. However, are the benefits that so many interviewees described really inherent to monogamy? Many nonmonogamous individuals described the benefits of their relationships in terms similar to those monogamists used—problematizing the uniqueness supposedly characteristic of dual fidelity and strict monogamy.

Comparing the perceived benefits and limitations of monogamy highlighted a certain sense of comfort and dependability in being monogamous and in not really having to articulate the need or desire for monogamy. It was as if a majority of the strict monogamists did not think (or need to think) about the alternatives to monogamy. Gay and bisexual men, as well as bisexual women, were more likely to choose or establish (rather than assume) monogamy, in part because many were aware of and had experience with alternatives to the master template. This could be a result of the historical exclusion of lesbian, gay, and bisexual individuals from legal same-sex marriage. However, heterosexuals were the most likely to emphasize the benefits of monogamy and being able to depend on dual fidelity for their relationships. The preceding interviewee examples and accounts introduce several key points of discussion in terms of whether it is the dyadic design of monogamy, the dual fidelity inherent in monogamy, or the resulting commitment that provides the benefits of strict monogamy.

Perhaps the most important benefit lies in what dual fidelity provides to those involved in strict monogamy. Sexual fidelity has malleable qualities that, whether secretive or consensual, are not sufficient to shake the supremacy of monogamy. Even though a number of interviewees articulated a history of cheating and engaging in extradyadic relations and veiled fidelity, they remained resolute in identifying as monogamous. What remains unclear is whether this refers to traditional monogamy or to a more contemporary version that includes softened sexual boundaries that better fit individuals' needs and desires while upholding emotional fidelity.

PERCEPTIONS AND DEMONSTRATIONS OF LOVE

Love remains a central theme in the discourse on monogamy and the master marriage template. Though romantic marriage is a relatively recent phenomenon, most relationships today involve an affective quality characterized as being in love with or loving one's partner. Love, like monogamy, is conceptual and subjective, although an enormous amount of attention has been given to theorizing, characterizing, researching, measuring, and problematizing love (Blumstein and Schwartz 1983; Cancian 1987; Evans 1993; Hatfield and Rapson 2005).

Interviewees were asked how they defined romantic love and subsequently asked how they showed love to their partners. Overall, most described love as an intense feeling, like butterflies in the stomach, that involves putting the other person's needs first, as well as being honest and open, and is often unconditional. Consider the following definitions of love:

I define love as closeness, not necessarily physically intimate, but maybe intimacy in other ways and also the support, openness, honesty, and loyalty between two people.

—Kandy, 19, heterosexual

I believe that love is an emotion that transcends companionship and the feelings associated with wanting to be with someone, whether it's with family or with a partner. It involves trusting someone to the point of being vulnerable, placing your life in their hands and not having to worry that the person will hurt you. Love is unconditional and there is no explanation for what love really means because love involves so many different levels and has so many different emotions.

—Wanda, 23, bisexual

Uh, well, love is when you'd do anything for someone and you want to be with them more than everyone else. And, in my estimation, it would be long term.

—Ronney, 21, heterosexual

I think love is when you put that person before you. Romantic love to me means you'll probably do anything for that person in terms of whatever they needed. The person you love is your other half.

—Grace, 21, heterosexual

Love is ... love is a strong word. I define love as the feeling you get when you see that certain someone, and no matter how many times you see that person, it's still like seeing them for the first time, like the whole butterfly in the stomach, kind of like, I guess, in the biological sense when your heart starts racing, and palms start sweating and just the feeling, the feeling of closeness you get by just being next to that person, and the whole, I guess, not to be sappy or anything, like how when they smile it warms you all up inside.

—Justin, 28, gay

These examples illustrate a variety of definitions that interviewees offered for love, although they were often preceded with a drawn out "uhmmm" and often followed by a statement like, "Wow—that's a good question, actually—I never really thought about it." There was little difference between how men and women, regardless of sexual orientation, defined love, although women were more likely to give lengthy definitions.

The characterization of love as being "between two people" was decidedly noticeable in a majority of responses. This ultimately reifies the assumption that romantic love is possible only within a dyad, an assumption that is preserved through dual fidelity and strict monogamy. In defining romantic love, strict monogamists illustrate that putting limits on loving more than one person romantically is not an option; it is simply not possible in their conceptualization of love. Falling in love with another person is, for monogamists, a "worst fear" and a clear violation of the fidelity and commitment between two people (see Halpern 1999 for a discussion of loving more than one person as a threat to normative relationships).

Interviewees were also asked how they showed love to their partners. Most were visibly excited to respond to this question—some sat up in their chairs, or their facial expressions would light up and they would smile brightly. Descriptions included showing love with "the little things"—calling every day, saying "I love you," making dinner, buying presents or treats, and cleaning the house. Others involved sexual favors or physically pleasing their partners:

> I make him dinner, call to say hello, spend time watching TV, you know—the little things; I think those little things are more meaningful than those big, extravagant-type deals.
> —Christopher, 20, gay

> I treat him to dinner and I'll buy him things to surprise him. Like there was this time he found a jacket in the store, so I went back

and got it for him. And I'll have sex with him to show him that I love him, even if I'm really tired [laughs].

—Melina, 23, heterosexual

By me being honest with him, and answering any of his questions honestly, I think I show him that my love is real and it's always there. And I'm not someone that's ever going to lie and betray him.

—Natalie, 32, bisexual

I have phone bills of two hundred dollars every month. So ... that's one way, by calling her. I also try to work towards our future. I just got an apartment for when she gets back [his girlfriend is studying abroad], and I've been taking 20 units at school and working a full-time job to save some money for us.

—Mike, 19, heterosexual

Well, primarily I express myself very physically with him. I like to pleasure him as much as I can. I tell him I love him whenever we're on the phone. I think it reassures him.

—Grace, 21, heterosexual

Although these descriptions of showing love vary in terms of doing "the little things" or even granting sexual favors, none includes a reference to sexual exclusivity or emotional fidelity. Yet a key characteristic of how strict monogamists view romantic love is that it is possible only between two people. This is why falling in love with another is experienced as threatening to the dyad.

Both men and women who varied in terms of sexual orientation similarly described doing "little things" for their partners to show their love. A number of younger heterosexual women described engaging sexually with their partners even if they were "tired" or "not really into it," behavior that seems less about giving sexual favors and more about overcoming fatigue or boredom. It also could involve focusing more on his sexual pleasure than on hers. Heterosexual men, in contrast, were more likely to describe showing love by providing financially, working hard, or being proactive about the future, as Ronney did. Gay and bisexual men, like bisexual women, offered ways of showing love that were similar to those mentioned by their heterosexual counterparts.

Some interviewees mentioned aspects of showing love that included "not betraying him/her" or "being committed," descriptions that speak to notions of faithfulness without explicitly articulating dual fidelity. In fact, Wade et al. (2009) found that demonstrations of love that exemplify (but do not necessarily overtly articulate) exclusivity were the most effective way to show a partner that one loves him or her, suggesting that exclusivity may be the most important goal of demonstrating love to another. For the strictly monogamous, showing love represents not only exclusivity but also fidelity in their relationships.

Establishing (?) Strict Monogamy

Only a few interviewees had in fact held a conversation in which they established monogamy in their relationships. They described simply assuming that the relationship would be monogamous and that the rules of monogamy (sexual and emotional exclusivity) were both understood and subsequently followed—no need to clarify or articulate one's expectations of dual fidelity. This is, of course, characteristic of mononormativity. The rules are so deeply socialized and institutionalized that there is no real need to state them. Strict monogamists therefore passively structure their relationships by assuming and relying upon socially normed dual fidelity. Consider the following interviewee comments about not actively establishing monogamy with their partners:

> I never even thought to have a conversation with Jules about being monogamous. I guess we just were from the start.
> —Marie, 31, heterosexual

> We never really talked about it. But we're monogamous.
> —Nigel, 21, heterosexual

We don't have an agreement but more of a mutual understanding that we won't have sex with other people.
—Natalie, 32, bisexual

We don't have set rules because that would put, I guess, a strain on the relationship, because that would be controlling. But we have more like, "unwritten rules" that, like, you don't hook up with other people, don't have sex with other people, just like I guess we assume that sort of stuff in a relationship.
—Mario, 22, heterosexual

For many strict monogamists, the rules of their relationships (dual fidelity) are assumed, implied, or unwritten—that is, not actively articulated. Mario's suggestion that an explicit agreement would "strain" the relationship is curious. This implies that having a conversation about monogamy might bring up the possibility of nonmonogamy or that articulated rules would be controlling, which could also be read as limiting. Ronney, a twenty-one-year-old heterosexual man dating his girlfriend of over a year, described the rules of monogamy as implied in his relationship. He suggested that an explicit agreement was unnecessary:

I think it's just kind of implicit that we are supposed to remain faithful to each other. It's the ideal relationship, and it's the same for both of us and that's what's going on. I don't think it is necessary to have an agreement, really. I think the standard is just to, you know, remain faithful, and it doesn't really need to be said. It's kind of understood by both sides.

The "standard" is, of course, dual fidelity patrolled through mononormativity. One interviewee related that he had not customarily talked about the rules of monogamy with his former girlfriends or even with his current wife. Edward, a forty-three-year-old heterosexual Mexican American man, had been married for three years:

Um, I've never talked about it [being monogamous]. I've had lots of relationships, so I've learned through a lot of past experiences that there is just no reason for a man who is in a very strict monogamous relationship to be alone with another woman. There really is no reason whatsoever, unless [pauses, focuses intently on one side of the table]—well, no. There is no reason in a personal environment. I mean, work is obviously different, but, um, and I knew that when I met my wife, and she knew that before we started dating and stuff like that. It wasn't that we talked about it; we both assumed it. I knew it, and I was pretty sure that she knew it, too.

Both Ronney and Edward, like others, described their agreements involving dual fidelity as implied and assumed because there is "just no reason" to articulate them with each other. Again, this speaks to the hegemony of monogamy that is perpetuated through social institutions and norms in American culture—and the assumption that one's partner is squarely on the same page. However, several "monogamists" in this study, because the rules were not explicitly stated or agreed upon, had broken them in some way; this is the focus of chapter 3. Further, the tension between chosen and implied monogamy is representative of individuals' struggles with their sexual agency and their awareness of various alternatives to the master template.

Sexual orientation was a determining factor in whether strict monogamists actively articulated the rules of dual fidelity. Gay and bisexual men were most likely to describe having held a conversation about being strictly monogamous and what that entailed. Again, this is probably due to the large number of gay and bisexual men who are engaged in or have had experience with nonmonogamy, given that the gay and bisexual male community has a long history of nonmonogamous (especially sexual) behavior.[1] Consciously and verbally choosing strict monogamy is more salient than assuming it for gay and bisexual men. For example, Brach and Dennis, gay men, had been together for over four years in a strictly monogamous relationship. I asked each if they had held a conversation about being monogamous, to which Brach replied:

Yeah, we did. Basically, once we got physical we said that we're really excited about this and we want to have each other for only each other and not share with anyone else. We wanted to be exclusive, and we don't want to have sex with anybody else. It was kind of like, we wanted to make sure that the other one knew that we weren't like our other friends, you know, who hook up and have group sex and stuff. We wanted to be monogamous.

Similarly, several bisexual women indicated that they had held an explicit conversation about being strictly monogamous because bisexuality introduces the possibility of wanting or needing multiple sexual partners of multiple genders. Joan, the previously introduced bisexual married woman, described a conversation she had with her husband when they were first married:

> I told my husband that I was bisexual two weeks into our relationship. He was fine with it. But I wanted to make sure that he knew that I was monogamous, and even though my bisexual friends were all involved in open marriages, I wanted to be monogamous with him. I think we were standing in the garage making something together and I brought it up.

Two strictly monogamous bisexual women (a demographic rather difficult to locate for the sample) were involved with heterosexual men and indicated that they had yet to have a conversation about being monogamous because they had no desire to be with other women. Instead of stating strict monogamy at the beginning of the relationship, they operated in terms of assuming and implying monogamy until a situation arose that necessitated an explicit conversation. These women were usually younger, had recently come out as bisexual, and had often been with their primary partner for less than a year.

Both heterosexual women and men operated under assumed or implied monogamy involving dual fidelity. This is not really surprising given heterosexual mononormativity. There were several differences between heterosexual men and heterosexual women. When asked about any conversations or stated agreements about monogamy, most heterosexual men responded that they simply assumed that they were in strictly monogamous relationships. This could be a reflection of male sexual scripts that involve less overt communication, or it could be an indication of the inherent patriarchy of the master marriage template. It may also provide a fallback for some heterosexual men who break the rules of monogamy by cheating—as in "Oh, I didn't know that wasn't allowed / we were that serious / we were monogamous."

Heterosexual women, however, indicated that rather than having held an explicit conversation, they had often *clarified* strict monogamy at different points in their relationships. One interviewee described this clarification process as a result of having been cheated on by her first boyfriend. When she started dating her current boyfriend, she wanted to clarify her expectations of monogamy; however, she never had a formal conversation with him. She made comments here and there to him about "being just us" and "not having to use condoms, because we're together, right?" This, of course, could be a reflection of women's sexual scripts that involve a more passive approach to communicating boundaries and expectations. Or it may indicate fear that if a woman actively establishes strict monogamy, she may seem pushy or too demanding of commitment from her male partner.

An overwhelming number of monogamists indicated that they had never had a conversation about being strictly monogamous. This, again, is a reflection of mononormativity and the master marriage template. Interviewees described following the rules of dual fidelity because "that's how I was raised" or stated that "I expect the same from my partner," indicating that many had never really entertained alternatives or thought to choose differently. Further, those who had explicitly discussed strict monogamy were more aware of the alternatives to monogamy, more often gay or bisexual, and better able to articulate the benefits and limitations of being in a monogamous relationship.

Finally, I asked monogamous interviewees why they followed the rules of strict monogamy (which I clarified as being dual fidelity through sexual and emotional exclusivity), regardless of whether they were overtly stated (which was rare) or tacitly understood:

> It's a two-way road. What one person does to you, or doesn't do to you, I guess, you reciprocate it.
> —Alexander, 19, bisexual

> I believe in the rules. I believe that they are true, and I know that by following them I will be happy.
> —Edward, 43, heterosexual

> I, well, I guess we follow the rules because we know that it hurts each other's feelings if we don't. And you know it would make me really sad if I knew that he was hurting inside because of something he did to me, too.
> —Melina, 23, heterosexual

In describing why they followed the rules, some interviewees said that they did so because that is how they had been socialized. Several questions centered on whether the interviewee's parents, family members, and friends were monogamous, conveyed messages about monogamy, or advised against its alternatives. Strict monogamists were quick to point out that their parents "had no reason" *not* to be strictly monogamous, and most said that they were following in their family members' footsteps. Others related that they would hurt or betray their partner in some way if they did not follow the rules. Overall, among heterosexual men and women, a number responded with a perplexed look, stating that it was simply assumed that they would follow the rules. Most gay and bisexual men, as well as many bisexual women, discussed rules in the context of having to establish or identify the consequences of breaking them. Given that strict monogamists rarely establish explicit agreements about what monogamy means, dual fidelity is more passively assumed and expected through dyadic design.

Dual fidelity, therefore, remains the foundation of strictly monogamous relationships. Because monogamy is culturally and institutionally emphasized, it provides a benchmark of intimacy that most strive to achieve without needing to define it. In exploring how strict monogamists conceptualize monogamy, I found that many struggle with a definition but still know what monogamy means in terms of both sexual and emotional exclusivity. Although interviewees veered between assuming and explicating sex and love as components of dual fidelity, almost all described monogamy in dyadic terms. In other words, whatever sexual and emotional exclusivity, commitment, or fidelity is assumed or desired must happen between two individuals.

The sense of security that comes from subscribing to the social norm of monogamy is, according to interviewees, a main benefit of being monogamous. Other benefits include not having to worry about transmitting or contracting a sexually transmitted disease or infection from an outside partner, as well as being able to rely on the loyalty and commitment between two partners. However, interviewees also described limitations of monogamy in terms of its restricting sexual possibilities, controlling individual agency, rendering a bisexual identity invisible, fostering boredom, and furthering the notion that all one's emotional and sexual needs can and should be met by only one person. Regardless of its benefits and limitations, most assumed monogamy; only a few interviewees had actively *chosen* to be strictly monogamous.

Romantic love remains paramount in contemporary relationships, and perceptions and definitions of love are mononormative. Because strict monogamists subscribe to the notion that being in love is possible only between two individuals, such perceptions of love influence their assumptions, expectations, and engagement in dual fidelity. Further, interviewees described showing love to their partners through "the little things" rather than through sexual and emotional exclusivity, yet dual fidelity is predicated upon being in love with only one person.

Assumptions about both what monogamy means and in what context romantic love can occur result in couples who have not clearly articulated their needs or expectations regarding commitment, exclusivity, and the potential consequences for violating the rules of monogamy. Given that dual fidelity is assumed and implied rather than explicitly stated among strict monogamists, this has a direct effect on how contemporary monogamous relationships operate. Few strict monogamists have intentional discussions to determine sexual or emotional exclusivity, relationship rules, or even the consequences of rule violations. Individuals seldom explicitly agree upon monogamy or what monogamy entails when developing their relationships. Such assumptions of dual fidelity in relationships aptly illustrate the pervasiveness of mononormativity.

Examining how gender and sexual orientation influence perceptions of monogamy and romantic love illustrates that sexual scripts and relationship ideals are still fairly gendered and heteronormative. Data exploring dual fidelity in gay, lesbian, and bisexual relationships illustrate that although the cultural landscape of intimacies has in fact shifted, the master marriage template continues to engender and heterosexualize strict monogamists. Further, bisexual women and gay men tend to choose rather than assume strict monogamy as their main relationship form, due in part to the nature of bisexuality, as well as to nonmonogamous relationships' being more common in both gay male and bisexual communities. Heterosexual women are most likely to clarify (rather than assert) monogamy throughout the relationship, exemplifying gendered sexual scripts about commitment in heterosexual relationships.

The overall individual and cultural success of the master template involves assuming dual fidelity through monogamy. Though this is ultimately predicated upon marriage, most of the strict monogamists in this study were not married. Whereas the age of the sample is not representative of the American population, the research participants exemplify strict monogamy without the necessity of marriage. This indicates, perhaps, a departure from marriage as central to the master template and a move toward monogamy itself as the contemporary relationship standard. Dual fidelity, therefore, assumes the possibility of successful intimacy outside the marital context.

Strict monogamists follow the normative rules of monogamy; they are in love and have sexual relations with only each other. Dual fidelity, according to strict monogamists, provides commitment, loyalty, and security between romantic partners. The result is that strict monogamists feel significant in their relationships because they share love and sex with only each other; they are special to only each other through dyadic sexual and emotional exclusivity. Such significance or specialness shared between partners is the unexpected basis of this research; the following chapters demonstrate precisely how important it is to feel significant, to feel special, in a relationship—regardless of whether it is strictly monogamous, mostly monogamous, nonmonogamous, or polyamorous.

ENDNOTES

1. Gay men have been denied same-sex marriage rights, a fact that may affect the types of relationships common among gay men.

CHAPTER 3

"It Was Just Sex;
I Didn't Love Her"

Veiled Fidelity and Mostly Monogamy

Many self-identified monogamists adhere to the master template, but several interviewees in this study described a more nuanced form of practicing monogamy while ensuring fidelity. This chapter exposes the tension between ideology and practice involved in many contemporary relationships through examining those who identify as monogamous but do not, essentially, behave monogamously. Studies have focused on this tension in a primarily deviant context by examining rates of and reasons for cheating, by exploring the consequences of infidelity, and by assessing permissiveness of extramarital sex. Yet researchers have neglected to provide samples that include a range of relationship scenarios and possibilities, reinforcing a monogamous/promiscuous dichotomy rather than effectively assessing a continuum of commitment, behavior, and relationship identification. I refer to these individuals as *mostly monogamous* because they exemplify a further distinction between sex and love through their attempts to define sex and conceptualize cheating.

Because a paradox exists wherein individuals embrace the master template but behave differently, the literature has invoked a framework of secrecy, cheating, and deviance to examine this tension between the monogamy ideal and people's desires or behaviors. Further, therein lies the assumption that the opposite of fidelity is infidelity—in other words, that if individuals are not being faithful, they are being unfaithful. However, among the mostly monogamous, there is still commitment, loyalty, and essentially fidelity between partners; it is just not dual fidelity. I call this *veiled fidelity* because it is essentially an overt attempt to obscure the expectations of sexual and emotional exclusivity inherent in strict monogamy. Veiled fidelity is a digression from traditional tenets of strict monogamy; it becomes a context for reconciling individual sexual and emotional needs, as well as extradyadic behaviors, within conventional relationship templates. At times, veiled fidelity also maintains gendered privileges within other-sex relationships.

In examining veiled fidelity among the mostly monogamous, I argue that the definition of sex affects reporting rates, perceptions of, engagement in, and responses to extradyadic sexual contact. Defining sex has been a neglected point in examining intimate relationships due to the assumed delineation of penile–vaginal intercourse as sex. Descriptions of what constitutes sex (and therefore sexual interaction) in assessing both extradyadic permissiveness and behavior have relied upon a limited heterosexual definition of intercourse. For example, research indicates that oral–genital contact is not considered sex by as much as 59% of the population, and 19% do not consider penile–anal penetration to be sex (Sanders and Reinisch 1999; Risman and Schwartz 2002). What constitutes sex, therefore, affects what is considered cheating in monogamous relationships. Further, the fidelities characterizing contemporary relationships allow a more flexible approach to commitment through a reconsideration of what constitutes sex.

Survey and interview data with self-identified monogamists underscore that veiled fidelity involves a further distinction between sex and love in justifying, allowing, and responding to extradyadic behavior. Moreover, notions and expectations of the master template are gendered and vary in terms of sexual orientation. The mostly monogamous technically uphold the ideology of monogamy while modifying fidelity to fit their own narratives, desires, and behaviors, and this results in an emphasis on emotional exclusivity rather than on dual fidelity. Veiled fidelity becomes the catalyst to preserving and expressing commitment among the mostly monogamous; it allows individuals to feel significant in their relationships.

Given that strictly monogamous relationships are constructed by dyadic exclusivity, most individuals (as well as researchers) assume that fidelity is both sexual and emotional. The script of romantic relationships is widely understood as two people who fall in love and have sex with only each other. Traditionally, because sexual fidelity represents commitment to one's partner and is the foundation of monogamy, violating it should be the ultimate form of betrayal. Though this may be true for some, as evidenced by people who leave their partners because of sexual infidelity (see Treas and Giesen 2000), the results of this study show that enforcing contemporary monogamy seems to relate more to emotional fidelity than to sexual commitment. The data demonstrate this apparent variance from the ideal in two main circumstances: when monogamous people engage in or respond to cheating, and when monogamous individuals engage in or agree to engage in more covert extradyadic sexual relations while preserving commitment—for instance, through veiled fidelity. A key component in this variance is the way individuals define sex.

REINFORCING MONOGAMY AND FIDELITY BY (RE)DEFINING SEX

In addition to assuming the meaning of monogamy, individuals assume the definition of sex, as well as what "counts" as sex. Part of this adjustment correlates to general social trends in blurring the boundaries between what is sex and what is "sexual" (Risman and Schwartz 2002). In addition, gays and lesbians have effectively problematized the traditional definition of sex as vaginal–penile intercourse. For example, do two women who have sex with each other *really* have sex if there is no penis involved? Oral–genital contact is increasingly becoming a sexual act rather than actual sex (see Risman and Schwartz 2002). This shift has several determinants, which include reduced stigma and fear about sex and sexuality, as well as a general expansion in the repertoire of sexual interactions as a result of more knowledge of, comprehension of, and exposure to sex in general.

Researchers have identified a significant motivation in reconsidering sex for the purposes of remaining a virgin. Because virginity technically refers to someone who has not experienced sexual intercourse (read: vaginal intercourse), those who wish to retain their virginal status yet explore their sexual desires often engage in oral–genital contact, manual stimulation, and sometimes anal penetration (Sanders and Reinish 1999). In other words, because society emphasizes virginity through cultural, religious, and institutional norms, individuals have found a way around such restrictions through redefining sex in terms other than "intercourse" and "vaginal–penile penetration."

This study's survey data show that 96% of monogamous respondents considered vaginal penetration to be sex, and 78% considered anal penetration to be sex—compared to 68% who considered giving oral stimulation and 67% who considered receiving oral stimulation to be sex. These results are consistent with current research on sexual behavior; many, especially young adults, do not consider oral stimulation to be sex (Risman and Schwartz 2002; Hatfield and Rapson 2005). Further, 45% of respondents considered manual stimulation to be sex, and only 28% considered masturbation to be sex (table 2).

Table 2. Survey responses of entire sample and monogamists to "What do you consider 'sex'?"

	Total N=2218	Monogamous N=1363
Vaginal Penetration	95%	96%
Anal Penetration	82	78
Giving Oral Stimulation	71	68
Receiving Oral Stimulation	71	67
Use Hands for Stimulation	51	45
Self-Stimulation (Masturbation)	31	28

Whereas women and men tend to have varied approaches to intimacy, sex, and love—as indicated in sexual scripts, gender scripts, and experiences in relationships—monogamous women and men have fairly comparable definitions of sex. The only statistically significant relationship ($p < .05$) between gender and defining sex occurred with considering vaginal penetration as sex; the p value was significant at .000. Sexual orientation, however, was statistically significant across the board in terms of determining whether each type of behavior constitutes sex; each p value was either .000 or less than .05. First, though most men and women of all sexual orientations considered vaginal penetration to be sex, gay and bisexual men were the least likely to do so. Rather, gay and bisexual men were the most likely to consider anal penetration as sex, which may be a result of male—male bodily configurations and the absence of female genitalia in a majority of their sexual interactions. Lesbian women were more likely to consider both giving and receiving oral stimulation, as well as using hands for penetration, as sex.

Table 3. Monogamous survey responses to "What do you consider 'sex'?" by total gender and sexual orientation by gender.

	Total Women N=710	Lesbian Women N=92	Bisexual Women N=86	Straight Women N=520
Vaginal Penetration	98%	96%	97%	99%
Anal Penetration	76	79	83	74
Giving Oral Stimulation	69	91	76	63
Receiving Oral Stimulation	69	91	77	63
Use Hands for Stimulation	44	83	59	35
Self-Stimulation (Masturbation)	28	52	43	20

	Total Men N=647	Gay Men N=176	Bisexual Men N=21	Straight Men N=446
Vaginal Penetration	92%	80%	71%	98%
Anal Penetration	98	98	90	72
Giving Oral Stimulation	68	87	86	59
Receiving Oral Stimulation	66	84	76	58
Use Hands for Stimulation	45	64	67	36
Self-Stimulation (Masturbation)	28	44	52	20

Note: Queer/Other respondents were less than 1%

Heterosexual women were slightly more likely than heterosexual men were to consider giving and receiving oral stimulation as sex, whereas heterosexual men and women were least likely to consider self-stimulation as sex (table 3).

Interview data show a similar pattern in what is considered sex; respondents gave varied definitions that ranged from traditional intercourse to alternative definitions. When asked to define sex, Iain, a twenty-one-year-old heterosexual man, said, "I would probably have to say intercourse." Others gave similar definitions, such as "I think penetration counts as sex," or "Sex is vaginal intercourse." Jacinda's definition, although it incorporates intercourse, is more elaborate:

> I think sex is when two people have sexual intercourse. It can be more meaningful when you're with someone you care about, and if you just do it with someone random, then sex serves the purpose of just pleasure with no emotion.

Most interviewees, like the survey respondents, considered intercourse, vaginal penetration, and to a lesser extent anal penetration to be sex. However, also like the survey respondents, many interviewees did not consider oral–genital contact to be sex:

> I think pure intercourse counts as sex. I think anal intercourse also counts, but I don't think oral sex counts as sex.
> —Kandy, 19, heterosexual

> I definitely consider sex to be vaginal intercourse. Well, I think anal is sex, too. But not oral.
> —Ariel, 24, bisexual

> Intercourse would be the best way to describe sex. I wouldn't consider oral sex or masturbation or hand jobs or even blow jobs. I think it's the penetration between the penis and the vagina.
> —Edward, 43, heterosexual

Anal or vaginal is definitely how I define sex; I wouldn't define oral as sex, though. I think sex is an intimate thing, it has an intimate effect to your relationship; I think it's meaningful but it's also fun and pleasurable.

—Wanda, 23, bisexual

I'd consider anal penetration to be sex, but I don't think oral counts. Giving or receiving. My boyfriend may disagree, but that's what I think.

—Dennis, 34, gay

These accounts show that that many do in fact draw distinctions between oral–genital contact and that which involves vaginal or anal penetration, although some did consider oral–genital contact to be sex, like Melina: "Sex is any private physical encounter other than, like, kissing and I guess touching. It includes oral, fingering, and of course sexual intercourse."

The survey and interview data are consistent with other research on sexual behavior (Risman and Schwartz 2002) that documents a definition of sex that increasingly excludes oral–genital contact. Some researchers have pointed to the potential problems with this shift—for example, sexually transmitted infections can be spread through oral–genital contact; if people do not consider oral stimulation to be sex, they are less apt to use protection while engaging in such behavior.[1] Conversely, HIV transmission is not associated with oral sex, which may encourage oral–genital contact as a way to avoid high-risk behavior.

Same-sex sexual interactions have expanded the heteronormative definition of sex, which relies on penetration of female by male genitalia, resulting in more individualized, diverse definitions of sex. Further, it seems that a narrowing definition of "actual sex" is taking place, accompanied by a concurrent expanding of what is considered "sexual." This may allow more individuals to assert their sexual agency, draw personal distinctions, and engage in sexual behavior that does not necessarily need to involve vaginal or anal intercourse.

Many of the mostly monogamous strategically modify their definitions of sex in an attempt to negotiate veiled fidelity. In terms of monogamy, when individuals do not consider oral–genital stimulation to be sex, the implications are twofold. First, because sexual fidelity is based on sex, would engaging in extradyadic oral–genital contact constitute a breach? In other words, is having oral sex with someone else really cheating? Given that it would just be sex—or even merely "sort of" sex —without emotion or love, is it truly a severe infraction? Geary, a fifty-one-year-old gay man, demonstrated the relevance of these questions:

> Matt and I are monogamous; we don't have sex with other men. I've never cheated on him; I could never do that. I do occasionally give blow jobs to other guys, but that's not sex to me. I don't consider it cheating … it's just a blow job.

Second, because monogamy is emphasized and commonly recognized (recall Joan's reference in chapter 2 to everyone's knowing what monogamy means) and because cheating is not only a fear of many but also a reality, having an understanding that reinforces the *emotional* pair bond while allowing for certain extradyadic *sexual* contact through "not real sex" and that operates as veiled fidelity may be the more realistic description of the way contemporary monogamy functions. In other words, just as the definition of sex can accommodate sexual desire juxtaposed with an emphasis on virginity, it may also accommodate an increase in sexual behavior with others while maintaining an emphasis on monogamy through emotional rather than sexual fidelity.

CHEATING: THE SUPPOSED CONTRAVENTION OF MONOGAMY

Most research on secretive extradyadic relations has focused on reasons for cheating, repairing relationships damaged by infidelity, and assessing the significance of permissiveness toward extramarital relations. This study takes a slightly different approach to cheating by exploring how the definition of sex and the differentiation of sexual and emotional infidelity correspond to contemporary notions of monogamy and the desire to feel significant within a romantic relationship.

In the survey results from self-identified monogamous individuals, 22% admitted to having cheated on their current partners, compared to 9% who acknowledged that their partners had cheated on them (table 4).

Table 4. Survey respondents' reported rates of cheating in monogamous relationships.

Have You Cheated on Your Current Partner?

	Monogamous N=1363
Yes	22%
No	78
Refused to Answer	*

Has Your Current Partner Cheated on You?

	Monogamous N=1363
Yes	9%
No	90
Refused to Answer	*

*Less than 1%

These results are low compared to national averages, which suggest that a range of 15–50% of individuals have cheated on their current partners (see Davis and Smith 1991; Laumann et al. 1994; Treas and Giesen 2000). Perhaps this is due to underreporting based on unwillingness to respond honestly, fear of one's partner finding out, and difficulty assessing what constitutes cheating. Likewise, given that individuals do not always know whether their partners have been cheating, such percentages reflecting partner rates of cheating may be significantly higher in reality.[2]

Gender remains significant in determining rates of cheating on one's primary partner. Results indicate that, overall, more men (26%) than women (19%) have cheated on a current partner, which is statistically significant ($p = .017$). Although this number reflects a higher rate of cheating for men than for women, confirming the data in several other studies, that 19% of women have cheated on their partners indicates that secretive extradyadic relations are not strictly a male pattern. Further, although there is no statistical significance between rates of cheating and sexual orientation, results do show that cheating occurs regardless of sexual orientation (table 5).

Survey respondents were asked to indicate what behaviors they engaged in during the process of cheating on their primary partners. The main purpose of this question was to assess whether reported rates of cheating correlated with certain types of sexual or emotional interaction. Results indicate that of those who reported cheating, a majority had kissed (76%), received oral stimulation (40%), spent the night (35%), given oral stimulation (33%), engaged in vaginal penetration (33%), used hands for stimulation (29%), or engaged in anal sex (10%) with someone other than a primary partner. However, only 9% of respondents indicated that they had fallen in love while cheating on their partners.

Table 5. Monogamous survey respondents' cheating rates by gender and sexual orientation.

Have You Cheated on Your Current Partner?

	N	Yes	No
Total Women	710	19%	81%
Lesbian Women	92	17%	83%
Bisexual Women	86	22	78
Straight Women	520	18	82
Total Men	647	26%	74%
Gay Men	176	26%	74%
Bisexual Men	21	19	81
Straight Men	446	26	74

Has Your Current Partner Cheated on You?

	N	Yes	No
Total Women	710	9%	91%
Lesbian Women	92	10%	90%
Bisexual Women	86	14	86
Straight Women	520	9	91
Total Men	647	9%	91%
Gay Men	176	14%	86%
Bisexual Men	21	10	90
Straight Men	446	7	93

Note: Queer and Other respondents were less than 1%

When asked to indicate the consequences of cheating, survey respondents reported that in a majority of cheating cases, the primary partner never found out (56%). Because most of the cheating behaviors were sexual (e.g., kissing, oral stimulation, vaginal penetration) rather than emotional (e.g., falling in love), the notion of veiled fidelity in terms of maintaining emotional exclusivity becomes salient once again. For those who either admitted cheating or were found to have cheated, forgiveness (23%), nothing (17%), and other (6%)[3] were the most common consequences (table 6).

Breaking up occurred in only 6% of cheating cases. However, comparing what types of behavior led to breaking up, reveals a statistically significant relationship between those who fell in love with an extradyadic partner and a resulting breakup of the primary relationship for a certain period of time. Further, for those who engaged in sexual behavior, the most common response from the primary partner, if he or she found out, was forgiveness. These results illustrate, once again, that extradyadic sexual behavior, even though it is nonconsensual, is not as severe or threatening to the primary partner as extradyadic emotional involvement.

Interviewees further demonstrate the relevance of defining cheating; responses to and consequences of cheating are tempered by a deliberate distinction between sexual and emotional infidelity. Of the in-depth interviewees, many (38%) admitted to having cheated on their current partners, whereas several (12%) discussed having been cheated on by their partners. The main purpose of engaging in a dialogue on cheating with the interviewees was to more fully assess any differences between sexual and emotional fidelity, explore the role of gender and sexual orientation in cheating rates and responses to it, and determine whether there were variations in consequences and accounts based on type of cheating behavior.

Table 6. Consequences of cheating as reported by monogamous survey respondents.

Cheated on Partner

	Total N=553	Monogamous N=298
Break up/divorce	5%	6%
Was forgiven	25	23
He/She never found out	46	56
Unsure	n/a	n/a
Nothing happened	12	7
Closed the open relationship	1	*
Other	10	6
Refused to answer	1	1

Was Cheated on By Partner

	Total N=300	Monogamous N=124
Break up/divorce	15%	20%
Was forgiven	51	53
He/She never found out	n/a	n/a
Unsure	3	3
Nothing happened	17	10
Closed the open relationship	2	2
Other	10	10
Refused to answer	1	2

*Less than 1%

Overall, the interviewees were open to speaking about cheating experiences. One couple in particular exemplified the nuances of cheating in their monogamous relationship. Justin, a twenty-eight-year-old gay man, had been with Marcus, a forty-three-year-old business entrepreneur, for over two years. Justin and Marcus were interviewed for this research separately, and both touted their success with and reverence for monogamy during their initial interviews. However, during a follow-up interview, Justin admitted to having cheated on Marcus:

> Marcus was in Chicago working on a project, so, you know, I was alone. It had been a hard week; I wasn't sleeping or eating well. I was on MySpace chatting with this guy I had met at the bar the night before and he kept AIMing me, saying he just wanted someone to fall asleep next to. So I invited him over but we didn't have sex. It felt really nice to have someone there. He asked if he could kiss me on the lips, and I said yes. This is where I considered it cheating. He started kissing me, and then we just talked together, and then it was just jacking off, and after that we did cuddle and fell asleep.

I asked Justin whether he had ever told Marcus about his actions:

> I called Marcus the next morning. I felt horrible, and I still feel horrible. I called him and said I wanted to let you know this happened and I'm driving away from this guy's house right now and we did jack off a bit. After a while, he told me about two prior instances where he got a massage and the guy ended up giving him a hand job. He knows I love him and this was just about getting off. That's it. Just a hookup, you know?

Justin's emphasis on his extradyadic behavior as mainly sexual rather than emotional suggests, once again, that sexual violations are less severe than those that involve feelings.[4] However, Justin did relate that he had been having a difficult week and felt alone because Marcus was gone—and ended up talking, cuddling, and falling asleep with "the guy." Such behavior seems emotionally intimate, although Justin did not describe it as such. Yet what he admitted to Marcus on the phone the next day was a sexual rather than an emotional violation ("jack off a bit"). Many interviewees offered similar accounts and distinguished between different types of cheating, as Grace (previously introduced) did:

> Cheating occurs in different levels. There's cheating physically, emotionally, and maybe even mentally. Mental would be that there's somebody that's there who you rely on more than your partner. Physically, well, obviously engaging in sexual acts. Maybe even intimate acts. Emotionally, if you feel that you're not there, like if your heart was devoted to someone else. To me that's the worst, you know? Falling in love with someone else.

Marie, a thirty-one-year-old Mexican American woman involved with her boyfriend, Jorge, of two and a half years, disclosed distinctions similar to Grace's about cheating. When asked if she had ever cheated on her current partner, Marie replied,

> Physically no, but emotionally, yes. I started talking to someone else more than I was talking to my boyfriend. We would flirt on the telephone and send each other funny emails. It never went further than that, but in my heart I knew it was cheating. I know if he did that to me, I'd feel like it was cheating.

Interviewees offered accounts similar to Grace's and Marie's—such as "It was just sex; I didn't love her," "We just messed around," and "I forgave her because she didn't love the guy"—when reflecting on incidents of cheating. Although cheating is rarely, if ever, a favorable experience, sexual indiscretions are more commonly overlooked, justified, and forgiven than emotional indiscretions are.

A few articulated a common perception in terms of the effect of cheating on monogamous relationships. Jacinda, a bisexual twenty-year-old college chemistry major, said this:

> Everyone, well, almost everyone cheats at some point. Guys are gonna cheat no matter what. And, you know what, a lot of girls I know cheat, too. I guess I just think about it in terms of sex.

Guys need sex. It hurts me that Nick wants to have sex with other girls sometimes, but you know what? He loves me and that's what really matters. At least he tells me he loves me. Well, he loves me, and he says that just because he wants to fuck another girl sometimes that doesn't mean he doesn't love me. It just means he likes sex [laughs]. Lots of sex.

Jacinda's comment segues into the role of gender and extradyadic behavior. Because cheating has been traditionally attributed to men rather than women, there are pervasive cultural narratives that maintain "all men cheat," invoking biological justification for uncontrollable sexual urges or the male need to "reproduce and propagate the species" (Barash and Lipton 2001). Other researchers have found similar perceptions of the inevitability of cheating and gender differences in who is more likely to cheat (Blumstein and Schwartz 1983; Laumann et al. 1994). However, there is only a 7% difference in the number of men who reported cheating and the number of women who did so in this study. Perhaps this is a result of more women's realizing and exercising their sexual agency, given that the rates of infidelity among women have continued to rise (Atwater 1982; Hatfield and Rapson 2005). This may also be a result of an increase in self-reporting of extradyadic behavior, whereas in the past women were tight lipped about such involvements. Indeed, several studies have concluded that as more women have entered the paid workforce, started using the Internet, and become sexually empowered, opportunities for extradyadic behavior among women have increased (Atwater 1982; Barash and Lipton 2001).

The question remains: If cheating is such a problem in monogamous relationships and is seemingly unavoidable, why has sexual fidelity remained the marker of monogamy? It seems as though cheating is integral to the monogamous terrain; it is fearfully anticipated, it often transpires, and it is both rationalized and denied through individual definitions of sex.[5]

Some have made peace with this tension between a monogamous identity and involvement in secretive extradyadic sex through elaborate accounting schemes, such as Jacinda's comments that "just sex" does not really count as cheating and that "he loves me, and that's what really matters." Stressing emotional fidelity rather than sexual fidelity, Jacinda, like many of the interviewees and survey respondents, attempted to reconcile cheating into the framework of contemporary monogamy, dismissing its severity by distinguishing between love and sex. The result is a mostly monogamous relationship wherein dual fidelity has been replaced with veiled fidelity: a form of loyalty that looks like sexual and emotional exclusivity but operates more as emotional dyadic commitment.

One interviewee spoke of her solution to problems with cheating. Brandi, a vivacious twenty-one-year-old heterosexual woman married to her husband of three years, shared the following:

> I got married to Benjamin really young, like when I was eighteen. I was his first girlfriend, his first, you know, sexual experience. And let's just say I have had a few other guys before him. So I actually have been encouraging Ben to have sex with this girl at his work. It sounds strange—but I would rather have him have sex with her now with my permission than have him cheat on me behind my back. And she's cool. I don't think he'd fall in love with her, so she'd be a safe bet.

Brandi's proactive approach to cheating parallels several other interviewees' accounts of certain agreements or understandings that allow them to engage in various sexual behaviors with others while maintaining their monogamous relationships. Sometimes these arrangements are meant primarily to circumvent cheating, as in Brandi's case, whereas other times they offer the opportunity to experience group sex (e.g., threesomes), satisfy sexual needs or curiosities, or show trust between partners. Because these individuals still consider themselves monogamous, though they give or receive permission to be extradyadically sexual, again, the concept of fidelity retains its value while being obscured by sexual permissiveness.

During a supplemental interview I asked Rena, a thirty-eight-year-old lesbian, whether she had ever cheated on her wife of ten years, Celeste. She replied, "Well, it depends on what you consider cheating" and subsequently said that she and Celeste were monogamous. However, Rena later disclosed that she had, in fact, had several partners "on the side" that Celeste, age forty-one, had not found out about. The night before the interview, Rena had been out at a local gay club; she recounted her previous night's festivities with pride:

> So I was out alone at the [gay] bar last night for the first time in, like, six months. Girl, let me tell you I was feeling good! I ran into this *mamacita* that I always crushed on. Hadn't seen her in forever! I mean years. Before I got married to Celeste. We were dancing and kissing ... flirting ... and at bar time she asked for a ride home. I knew she didn't, you know, want just a ride [laughs]. While we were driving, we were catching up and I told her that Celeste and I had gotten married. She freaked out and was all, "Oh my god you're married—we can't be doin' this!" I said, "Look. I've done this friends with benefits thing before. It's not a big deal. Here are the rules: no drama, no feelings, no fallin' in love; keep it on the down low ... Well, we went down to her apartment and, you know, I let my freak flag fly! ... I think she's cool; she'll keep her mouth shut, so it's all good.

Rena said that she wished she could have an open relationship of some sort and struggled with Celeste's desire to be monogamous. From the start of their relationship, Celeste had been strongly opposed to any type of nonmonogamy, especially if Rena made a special request for a threesome or nonchalantly introduced a potential partner while they were at the bar. Eventually, Rena adopted a strictly monogamous approach to their relationship, stating that it was for the best that they were exclusive and that it would have hurt Celeste too much if she engaged in "shit on the side." However, a few years into their marriage, Celeste began a covert sexual and emotional relationship with a mutual friend. When Rena found out, she was crushed, jealous, and furious that her earlier requests for multiple-partner experiences had not been honored. She subsequently decided on her own that she would not necessarily pursue external partners, but if an opportunity arose, she would take it. Rena felt that because Celeste had cheated on her, she could no longer be strictly monogamous because Celeste wanted it; in a sense, she felt entitled to be sexual with other women. Rena did not consider this behavior cheating, however, because she did not actively seek out other women and because she kept the extradyadic behavior sexual. Rena's rules exemplify a distinction between having sex and falling in love, again reinforcing the importance of fidelity through emotional exclusivity.

Distinguishing Sex and Love to Preserve Commitment through Veiled Fidelity

Consent is an integral yet often overlooked concept in assessing extradyadic sexual relations. Because most researchers assume behavior with others to be secretive and nonconsensual, few have been able to accurately investigate situations in which partners allow each other through formal or informal agreements to engage in extradyadic sexual relations. This omission is indicative of hegemonic mononormativity and of an inability to conceptualize committed relationships as involving variations of sexual or emotional exclusivity.

A main purpose of the survey in this study was therefore to assess such situations and agreements. Respondents were asked what types of activity they "allowed" their primary partner to engage in with others. Respondents were then asked what types of activity they were "allowed" to engage in with others.

Figure 5. Percentage of monogamous survey respondents indicating allowable/allowed activities with others.

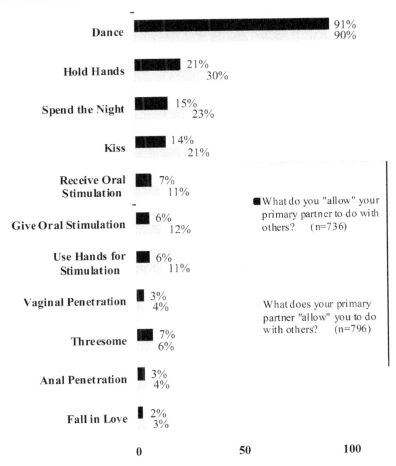

Though respondents identified as monogamous, many had given permission to (as indicated by the first percentage) and had been given permission by (as indicated by the second percentage) their partners to dance with (91%, 90%), hold hands with (21%, 30%), spend the night with (15%,

23%), and kiss (14%, 21%) other people. This may seem understandable given that dancing with and even kissing others could be seen as friendly or nonthreatening to the dual fidelity in a strictly monogamous relationship; however, some respondents reported that they allowed their partners and were allowed to give oral stimulation (6%, 12%), receive oral stimulation (7%, 11%), use hands for stimulation (6%, 11%), engage in vaginal penetration (3%, 4%), engage in threesomes or other group sex (7%, 6%), and engage in anal penetration (3%, 4%; figure 5).

These permissive activities explicitly violate the traditional standard of dual fidelity inherent in monogamy, yet respondents continued to identify as monogamous. The cardinal rule of sexual fidelity may be more malleable than previously thought, especially in terms of giving and receiving oral sex. Further, because monogamy is socially approved, even revered, identifying as monogamous may be more important than behaving monogamously.

In addition, the survey results can be interpreted several ways: first, monogamous individuals are allowing engagement in or being allowed to engage in oral sex, vaginal sex, group sex, and anal sex with others; however, falling in love with another is the most restricted activity. This pattern aligns with the previously discussed survey results on types and severity of cheating behaviors.

Moreover, survey data show a pattern wherein the respondent is allowed more freedom to engage in activities than the respondent's partner is, with the exception of dancing and threesomes. These flexible schemas can be self-serving, in that a respondent assumes that he or she has more freedom than his or her partner and therefore acts accordingly. This could also signify a sort of "I can do it, but he/she cannot" mentality that privileges the respondent's needs and desires rather than those of the respondent's partner.

In mostly monogamous relationships, sexual fidelity may be more flexible, but emotional fidelity remains most significant. Additionally, to account for the small percentage of monogamous individuals who allow their partners or are allowed to fall in love, perhaps sexual fidelity remains important, whereas falling in love is merely emotional rather than physical, underscoring the significance of sexual fidelity as a cardinal rule of monogamy.

Several interviewees were in fact mostly monogamous rather than strictly monogamous. Chapter 2 discusses those who subscribe in both ideology and behavior to strict monogamy, upholding dual fidelity. Melina, a twenty-three-year-old Mexican American woman in an eighteen-month relationship with her boyfriend, José, indicated that she and José were strictly monogamous, as the rules of the relationship indicate:

> We're not supposed to dance with anyone else when we go out to clubs. I mean, in our relationship we sort of know that the only people we can dance with is our mutual friends, and that's it. He also shouldn't check out girls, like, especially if we're together.

Melina represents the strictly monogamous relationship. However, a number of interviewees indicated a different approach to monogamy that involves extradyadic sexual relations. Such behavior, according to the interviewees, is not considered cheating because an agreement or understanding exists about what is or is not permissible conduct. That such behavior even occurs challenges the fundamental framework of monogamy; sexual and emotional exclusivity are the idealized tenets of intimacy. Nevertheless, several described allowing and being allowed by their partners to engage in various relations with other people but still identified their relationships as monogamous.

I asked each interviewee to describe any agreements they had with their partners about extradyadic relations. The agreements varied as to what behaviors were allowed or not allowed with others. For some, dancing was fine; for a few kissing, oral sex, or hand jobs were freely permitted. Ronney, a twenty-one-year-old straight man, had been dating a woman, Aurora, for over a year. Ronney described their agreement to not have sex with other people but said that Aurora was free to engage in dancing and kissing: "She can dance with other people; just my one rule was no grinding ... *no grinding*! And it's fine with me if she kisses guys, just not on the lips with tongue ... *no tongue!*" Ronney and Aurora have what many would consider a strictly monogamous relationship. However, because dancing and kissing have traditionally been shared between primary partners, allowing such activities with others moves the relationship into a more flexible context.

Several, like Tannah, have an even more tailored relationship that presents as mostly monogamous. Tannah, a twenty-year-old woman, had been dating her boyfriend for several months. She related that they had recently made their relationship exclusive, although she had given him permission to receive oral sex from other girls:

> I'd feel comfortable with Tommy getting head from another girl since I really don't like doing it [crinkles her nose]. But he can't, like, have sex with her. He can just get a blow job. I mean, guys love that shit, and I really hate doing it. And as long as he comes home to me at the end of the night, I'm fine ... Is that wrong? That sounds so horrible! I don't know [shrugs her shoulders].

Tannah later said that if she did not let Tommy receive oral sex from someone, he might want to cheat on her because she does not enjoy giving oral sex. This is reminiscent of comments made by Brandi, the previously introduced woman who encouraged her husband to have sex with his coworker so that he would not cheat on her later on. It seems as though one aspect to being mostly monogamous is preventative in terms of not wanting to hurt or be hurt by more secretive, destructive kinds of extradyadic relations. In this process, veiled fidelity becomes the assurance that emotional exclusivity is preserved and even that a certain form of sexual fidelity is preserved, depending on one's conceptualization of sex. Allowing or engaging in oral stimulation is therefore a compromise in meeting sexual needs without negatively affecting a primary bond between partners.

Martha, a thirty-four-year-old bisexual woman involved with her boyfriend, Thom, stated that her attitude on relations with others had recently become more serious:

> We have an unspoken rule 'cause we always joke around that oh, you are keeping your options open. I myself don't feel comfortable having sex with other people right now, although in the beginning I was seeing other people. My feelings just got to the point where I was really into him, and I still am. I know he is into me, but I think if he had the opportunity to have sex with another girl, he'd take it. It's fine with me because I know that his feelings are strong for me right now, too. It'd just be sex, you know? Like, just hooking up.

Martha's account introduces a temporal dimension to the strength and seriousness of emotional connectedness, describing the increasing intensity of her feelings for Thom and Thom's feelings for her as "strong for me right now." This suggests that veiled fidelity may, for some, serve as a temporary step in moving toward strict monogamy, or that it may operate as a step in the opposite direction, toward a more nonmonogamous relationship.

Devin, a twenty-five-year-old gay-bisexual man involved in a three-year monogamous relationship with his partner, Douglass, commented on his veiled fidelity as involving permission for group sex:

> So Douglass and I have an agreement about having sex together with other people. As long as I'm in the room or he's in the room, preferably participating, you know, then it's just fine. We don't have anal sex with other guys, but everything else is fine—you know, the usual. So we have a lot of threesomes and sometimes I have sex while Douglass watches, and vice versa. It's really hot, you know [laughs]? In fact, sometimes we use it to get each other off when we're alone. Like I'll describe how I enjoyed watching him with a particular guy.

I asked Devin why he identified his relationship as monogamous if he and Douglass frequently engaged in threesomes with other men. He replied, "I love Douglass so, so much. And we've been together for over three years now, living together for almost a year. He is everything to me. He's the one I love. That's monogamy to me." These interviewee accounts provide valuable insight into how contemporary monogamy operates through modified versions of fidelity; however, they fall short in addressing why individuals embrace monogamy while simultaneously creating elaborate accounting schemes to escape the expectations of dual fidelity.

Based on both survey and interview data, several suppositions can be made regarding veiled fidelity. First, although interviewees were quick to acknowledge that their agreements were mutual, there were still feelings of jealousy, inadequacy, and almost a bittersweet "if you can't beat 'em, join 'em" attitude about extradyadic relations. Some suggested that rather than discovering their partner's secretive sexual indiscretions, they preferred to encourage certain types of low-risk sexual behavior (like oral sex). Second, although Brandi, like several others, relied on veiled fidelity to persuade her husband to engage in sex with his coworker to avoid future problems with cheating, such attempts were not always successful in preventing more involved interactions. For example, even though Devin and Douglass were mostly monogamous and found manual and oral stimulation with others acceptable, later in Devin's interview, he disclosed that he engaged in regular hookups with other men that Douglass did not know about:

> I have a couple guys I see on a regular basis. Sometimes we jack each other off, sometimes I give them head, sometimes I get head. There's one guy I had anal with, but I don't usually do that. It's not that I don't love Douglass and enjoy the threesomes we have, I just need to get off more than he does, that's all ... He'd be really pissed if he found out.

Examining which behaviors are allowed and not allowed with others for those in mostly monogamous relationships reveals what appears to be a distinction between sex and love. Both survey and interview respondents stressed the importance of emotional fidelity while allowing or engaging in various sexual experiences with others, indicating that monogamy has not been completely reinvented. Rather, instead of focusing on dual fidelity as the primary indicator of loyalty, devotion, and commitment between individuals, veiled fidelity preserves emotional exclusivity while expanding the parameters of sexual desire and possibilities.

A final characteristic of veiled fidelity invokes a more individualized quality of commitment to one's partner. Although the mostly monogamous may have understandings or even agreements about what is allowed or not allowed with others, a number also maintain veiled fidelity through more individually imposed boundaries. The result is an "ethical cheating" that preserves emotional fidelity and even attempts to protect sexual fidelity by engaging in "not really sex" activities. One particular interview discussion about cheating with Hermes, a thirty-two-year-old heterosexual man planning to propose to his girlfriend of two years, Dana, exemplified this more individual approach to veiled fidelity:

> **Hermes:** I was a player before I met Dana. She's the most beautiful girl in the world. She's so amazing. And for the first time in my life, I wanted to get married. I've been really good with her, you know, like I never cheated on her. So, one night, this woman walks into my work, and she was just, you know, just fucking hot. She was really cool, too. We ended up hanging out after my shift ended. So, one thing led to another, and she ended up giving me head ... It would crush Dana. I should have never done it, but I was drinking and—I—I just couldn't resist. And the girl gave amazing head, too [laughs]. I mean, we became friends because she came into my work off and on.
> **Interviewer:** Did anything ever happen with her again?

Hermes: Um... [hesitates]. God, I must sound like a total prick. It's not like that. It—well, I tried to keep it just oral. Like I said, you know, she gave great head and Dana is just not that skilled in that area. She actually doesn't like it very much. But later on we did actually have sex one time [pauses and takes a deep breath]. I just felt so dirty afterwards. Not because of her, just because of me. It actually messed me up for a while because I never wanted to hurt Dana. I never thought I'd let it go that far.

I asked Hermes why he had engaged in oral sex with the girl in the first place, to which he replied, "It was just oral, you know, just to get off." For Hermes, drawing a personal boundary between oral stimulation to have an orgasm and penetrative sex that might involve a more emotional or meaningful purpose became the key to his narrative of keeping his commitment to Dana through veiled fidelity. His experience further underscores the tension between wanting to be monogamous and wanting simultaneously to fulfill sexual desires or meet sexual needs. After concluding the interview, Hermes and I had a more casual conversation about "the girl":

Hermes: The last time I saw her, we ended up hanging out after work again. I think by that time she knew about Dana, and was trying to be respectful, you know? But we also had a sort of chemistry or whatever. I was sitting on the step, and she leaned in to kiss me. We kissed for a while, and then I stopped. She asked me what was wrong, you know, 'cause I had never stopped before. I told her that I was trying to be good, and that I didn't want to hurt Dana.
Interviewer: How did she respond?
Hermes: She was actually really cool. She understood. She said, "Well, then I should go." ... It was hard. I liked her and enjoyed hanging out. And, like I said, you know, she was great at it. I think I grabbed her arm and said something like, "Not so fast." We sat there for a long time and talked. I just struggled with it because, I mean, at the end of the day, it's making a decision between what's right and what I want. You know?
Interviewer: So what did you end up doing?

Hermes: Well, I made the decision in my mind that I was just going to get oral from her and that was it. I like the way she sucks my cock, and she likes to suck it, so, you know, hey. I think after our conversation, she knew that I didn't want to actually have sex, just oral. So, you know, we did our thing.

Hermes's account highlights several issues in mostly monogamous relationships. First, in his conceptualization of oral stimulation as not really sex, Hermes demonstrated that defining sex is a component of negotiating contemporary relationships in terms of what is considered allowed, okay, or even cheating. Hermes did not think he was cheating on Dana until he had vaginal–penile sex with the other girl. Further, Hermes alluded to his sexual desire and to the fact that his girlfriend, Dana, was not good at and did not enjoy giving oral stimulation. For Hermes, receiving extradyadic oral sex was a justified solution for all parties involved, even the girl, who, he asserted, "liked to suck it." Whether this, in turn, compromised the girl's sexual satisfaction is a point of contention.

Finally, Hermes commented that he ultimately had to make a decision between what was right and what he wanted. Herein lies the paradox: in strictly monogamous relationships, what is right (dual fidelity) is, for the most part, upheld through wanting to do what is right, actually doing what is right, and resisting violating what is right for the sake of one's partner and the primary bond. However, mostly monogamous individuals have attempted to characterize their relationships as right while exploring, expanding, or fulfilling particular desires or needs through veiled fidelity. As Hermes and other interviewees aptly described, drawing boundaries between different types of sexual interaction and actual sex is a key component of veiled fidelity and informs what is considered cheating or "going too far," which may result in negative consequences. Even though Hermes had not had a conversation with Dana, in his mind he drew the boundary between oral sex and vaginal penetration and even justified his actions in terms of simply having an orgasm. In doing so, Hermes demonstrated his commitment to Dana through veiled fidelity and by behaving as mostly monogamous.

The continued valorization of monogamy coincides with evidence of behavior that seems inherently contradictory to its very definition. Given that traditional monogamy implies both sexual and emotional fidelity, there has been little need to explicate what monogamy entails. Though monogamy remains the master template, at the same time data illustrate that behaving monogamously fluctuates within blurred sexual and emotional parameters.

In addition, contemporary definitions of sex are indicative of a changing culture that though sexually savvy, resorts to a strategically limited description of what constitutes sex in order to (1) participate in sexual behaviors (but not sex) with others while continuing to identify as monogamous, and (2) engage in extradyadic sexual relations without considering such behavior cheating. This manipulation of sexual definition may seem furtive, but it operates in a manner comparable to individuals' efforts to retain their virginal status in a culture that stresses virginity. In other words, monogamy is the norm, and essentially these individuals are monogamous, even though their behavior does not align with dual fidelity. The result is a mostly monogamous approach to intimate relationships that reinforces significance between partners.

In assessing what constitutes cheating and how individuals respond to cheating, the distinction between sex and emotion is further articulated. Survey data show that respondents who cheated on their partners most often engaged in sexual behaviors like oral stimulation or vaginal or anal penetration rather than falling in love. This demonstrates that emotional exclusivity remains central to veiled fidelity among the mostly monogamous. Interview data confirm these results, indicating that interviewees often excused cheating through accounting schemes that reduced emphasis on sexual exclusivity while heightening the importance of emotional exclusivity—such as "he just had sex with her" or "she didn't fall in love." On the contemporary landscape of love and intimacy, sexual violations are therefore less threatening than emotional violations. Through veiled fidelity, emotional commitment is preserved, whereas sexual desires and needs are understood, justified, and usually forgiven.

This distinction between sex and emotion for the sake of maintaining monogamy is also evident in veiled fidelity. Veiled fidelity demonstrates that individuals attempt to prevent cheating through an understanding about extradyadic activity or attempt to reconcile their desires within a monogamous framework that, by design, discourages sexual behavior with others. In a sense, the mostly monogamous use veiled fidelity both in a social sense and in an individual sense; to others, such relationships look like strict—therefore socially approved—monogamy. Behind the veil, however, is a quite different scenario. Some hide behind this obscuration in order to avoid complicating their conversations or judgment. Others find reassurance and a sense of loyalty and commitment on a more personal level; as long as one does not have "actual sex" or fall in love, fidelity is preserved. Veiled fidelity ultimately demonstrates the cultural strength and centrality of dual fidelity as individuals attempt to replicate the master template ideal with modifications. The next chapter builds upon further distinctions between sex and love, notions of fidelity and cheating, and agreements about other partners by examining self-identified nonmonogamists who deliberately resist the master template.

ENDNOTES

1. Although the definition of sex is perhaps becoming more limited, rape definitions in criminal law are growing more expansive, extending the parameters of sex to include more kinds of sexual activities between more types of people (e.g., marital rape; see Frank et al. 2007).
2. Although both the survey sample and interview pool range in age from eighteen to sixty-seven, rates of cheating are similar among each age range, at roughly 23% per age group.
3. "Other" responses included counseling, therapy, "we talked it through," trial separation, "we took a break," and "he had to buy me a new car."
4. Justin's definition of sex at the beginning of the interview was this: "Sex would be any activity involving ejaculation or anal penetration. Actually, it also includes any penetration of orifices in the body, oral sex, anal sex, or vaginal sex." However, when asked if he considered his interaction to be sex (given that his previous definition included "any activity involving ejaculation"), he replied, "Well ... I don't consider masturbation to be sex."
5. See Pepper Mint's theoretical discussion of the ways cheating and monogamy are inevitably related (Mint 2005).

CHAPTER 4

"Do Whatever; Just Don't Fall in Love"

Specified Fidelity and Nonmonogamy

Fidelity is still very much an important component of romantic relationships, even for those who consent to multiple partners. Whereas strict and mostly monogamous individuals subscribe to the ideology of monogamy, there remains, for the mostly monogamous, a differing behavioral pattern. This chapter examines those who have resisted the tenets of monogamy and explores how nonmonogamists arrange their relationships and negotiate the commitment customarily preserved through dual or veiled fidelity. If the monogamous master template ideally provides commitment, intimacy, and love between partners, how (if at all) do nonmonogamous relationships experience fidelity? How does nonmonogamy complicate—or clarify—the master template?

The rules of monogamy are rarely overtly negotiated; most monogamists passively structure their relationships by assuming dual fidelity. If individuals choose to engage in nonmonogamy, how (if at all) do they construct their relationships? Does the master template inform their choices? How exactly are rules established, what agreements do partners have, and are the rules ever broken? If so, what are the consequences of rule violations? Nonmonogamists indicate through agreements and rules that emotional rather than sexual exclusivity ensures commitment and preserves significance between partners. I call this *specified fidelity* because not only is there a deliberate distinction between sexual and emotional exclusivity, but it is usually verbalized or agreed upon by both partners rather than assumed or implied.

Though the rules of monogamy are in fact normed and institutionalized, there is no socially prescribed master template for engaging in nonmonogamy with multiple partners. These rules continue to serve as the master template of nonmonogamous relationships, offering the catalyst for commitment, love, and specialness that dual fidelity seemingly provides. In addition, nonmonogamists do, at times, break the rules. Data indicate that rule violations are usually handled by renegotiating the rules rather than breaking up the relationship. The result is a contemporary approach to loyalty that relies not on sexual exclusivity but rather on specified, negotiated, and often renegotiated regulations that discourage multiple romantic partners in order to ensure emotional exclusivity through specified fidelity.

Whereas monogamy relies upon, and thus remains, a socially approved master template involving dual fidelity, nonmonogamy is more flexible in operation. The participants in this study show that engaging in nonmonogamy requires a process of establishing nonmonogamy through agreements. These agreements involve creating rules, boundaries, and limitations that (1) govern behavior with other partners, (2) designate other partners, and (3) encourage or discourage disclosure between partners. Moreover, a fourth category of rules emerged: those that are self-imposed and do not require collaboration yet are often based on previous consensual arrangements with a particular partner.

Rules serve several functions, although the most salient for nonmonogamists is the need to feel special with a particular partner.

They indicate a specification that allows extradyadic sexual relations but restricts, in various capacities, emotional bonds with others. The result is commitment preserved through specified fidelity. Further, when rules are violated, consequences more often involve a renegotiation of the agreement rather than breaking up or separation, which signifies deliberate resistance to mononormative definitions and consequences of cheating.

ESTABLISHING NONMONOGAMY THROUGH FORMAL AGREEMENTS

Survey results from 512 nonmonogamists indicate that a majority (75%) had established of some sort of agreement about extradyadic activities. Most (33%) had a verbal agreement; others described their agreements as "don't ask, don't tell" (24%), case-by-case (7%), or written (1%). Although some indicated that they had "no agreement" (15%), open-ended survey responses reveal that many verbally discussed extradyadic activity before it occurred on a more ad hoc basis.

One of the most important characteristics of nonmonogamy involves the presence of an agreement concerning extradyadic behavior. As discussed in chapters 2 and 3, the rules of monogamy are implicitly ingrained through the master template; there are few, if any, formal agreements about monogamy that couples must articulate. Lacking such agreements is not necessarily problematic; in fact, having to overtly choose monogamy and establish what that entails, as I have shown, is the exception rather than the norm.

Nonmonogamy introduces the notion of multiple partners; thus, it is often perceived as lacking any sort of rules or structure. This perpetuates the conceptualization of nonmonogamists as engaging in promiscuity and wanton, free-for-all sexual and emotional relations. However, both survey respondents and interviewees indicated that regardless of whether a relationship began as nonmonogamous, gradually moved

from a monogamous to an open relationship, or involved multiple partners in some capacity, almost all nonmonogamists had taken the time to
establish some sort of agreement.

Although there were agreements in some mostly monogamous relationships, few were as elaborate in terms of design, rule specifica-
tions, and execution as nonmonogamous agreements. In chapter 5, I
discuss polyamory agreements as even more intricate than those of
nonmonogamists. There are also several differences in the types of
agreements that nonmonogamists and polyamorists create. For example,
in this study nonmonogamists tend to have case-by-case, verbal, or
"don't ask, don't tell" agreements, whereas polyamorists favor written
and verbal contracts or other kinds of agreements that encourage disclosure.

Establishing and renegotiating these agreements formalizes specified
fidelity in nonmonogamous relationships, often articulating a context
wherein allowed and restricted behaviors emphasize emotional exclusivity. Survey data indicate that nonmonogamists allowed their primary
partners (85%) and were allowed by their primary partners (85%) to
engage in sexual and sometimes nonsexual behavior with others. True
numbers may be slightly higher, however, because several indicated
through open-ended responses that they took issue with the word
allow, and others indicated that at that particular time, the relationship
was closed for a variety of reasons, although they still considered it
nonmonogamous.

Like monogamists, nonmonogamists were asked what types of
activity they "allowed" their primary partners to engage in with others.
Respondents were then asked what types of activity they were "allowed"
to engage in with others.

Figure 6. Percentage of nonmonogamous survey respondents indicating allowable/allowed activities with others.

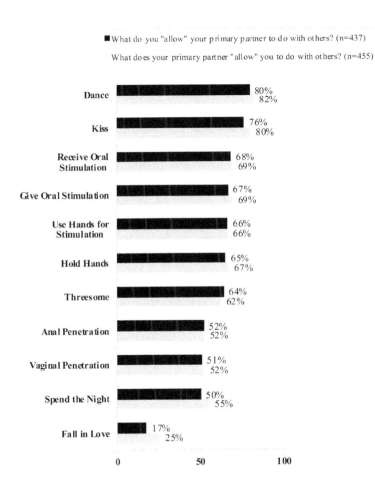

Results indicate that most nonmonogamists allowed their partners (as indicated by the first percentage) and were allowed by their partners (as indicated by the second percentage) to dance (80%, 82%), kiss (76%, 80%), receive oral stimulation (68%, 69%), give oral stimulation (67%, 69%), engage in vaginal penetration (51%, 52%), and engage in anal penetration (52%, 52%) and spend the night (50%, 55%). Even though several respondents allowed or were allowed by their partners to fall in love with another person, falling in love was the least acceptable interaction (17%, 25%; figure 6).

As individuals engage in nonmonogamy, many have no objection to outside sexual experiences, but few are comfortable with the idea of their partner's falling in love with another person. In fact, the distribution of allowable and allowed activities with others exemplifies a pattern similar to that found among monogamists; dancing is the most allowable interaction, and falling in love is the least allowable interaction, even among those who consider themselves nonmonogamous. Polyamorists also exhibit a fairly similar pattern regarding which activities are allowable or allowed.

In examining allowable or allowed activities within nonmonogamy, results once again underscore that sexual behaviors are not as commonly restricted as emotional relations. Interview data show that commitment and significance in nonmonogamous relationships is preserved through specified fidelity. Survey data show a pattern wherein nonmonogamists are allowed more freedom to engage in activities than their partners, with the exception of threesomes. A respondent may assume that he or she has more freedom than his or her partner does or demonstrate an "I can, but he/she cannot" attitude toward behaviors with others. There is, on average, a minimal difference between being allowed by and allowing one's partner to engage in such activities. This could be attributed to the agreements and rules that are mutually established between partners, which may help clarify what is acceptable behavior with others.

"It's Not a Free-for-All": Nonmonogamists' Rules, Boundaries, and Limitations

Interviewees indicated that their nonmonogamous relationships involved allowing or restricting certain activities with other partners. These activities were almost always designated through agreements about rules, boundaries, and limitations between primary and sometimes other partners. Although the rules cover a wide range of sexual and nonsexual activities, they can be classified in four main categories: rules governing behavior, rules designating other partners, rules regarding disclosure, and self-imposed rules.

Rules that Govern Sexual Behavior with Outside Partners

All nonmonogamous interviewees had explicit rules of some sort about which behaviors were appropriate or allowed with other partners. Rules about safe sex were of paramount concern, and interviewees typically responded as did Enrique, a nineteen-year-old gay man involved with two lovers: "Well, of course we have rules about safe sex—that's a given." There was no variation between genders or among sexual orientations; everyone had rules about barrier methods (e.g., condoms or dental dams), current test results (e.g., for HIV and other sexually transmitted diseases and infections), and disclosing accurate sexual histories (e.g., previous sexually transmitted diseases and infections, high-risk behaviors).

Although safety remains a central subject of rules, many interviewees had established additional rules governing sexual activities. Abbey, a twenty-seven-year-old bisexual woman, was involved in a ten-month relationship with a married man, Karl, who had several female lovers. Abbey described the rules that Karl's wife had imposed about behavior with other sexual partners: "There are three rules for Karl regarding relationships. One, no sex in their [marriage] bed; two, sex only if the kids are asleep; and three, he is not allowed to come inside me during vaginal sex." Kevin, a forty-four-year-old bisexual man, had been involved with several male and female lovers over twenty-three years and was currently partnered with a man and dating a few women. Kevin discussed the differences between his various partners' rules: "Each of my partners has different rules with me. Christine wants me to have oral sex with only her, and Zach's big thing is about safe sex. Johanna, well, she says anything goes, as long as I tell her after." While describing the rules among his different partners, Kevin became visibly upset and made a point of stopping the interview to relay the following:

> Do you know what pisses me off the most about this whole issue of monogamy versus nonmonogamy? Maybe I'm just being sensitive because I'm a bi male and I have to defend my position being caught in the middle ... or that people think bisexuals will literally fuck anything that moves or has a wet hole. I have standards. And I have rules with my partners. It's not a free-for-all. Married heteros cheat, have sex parties, and are dishonest with each other all the time. But the minute people think of bis and gays, they think *we're* the perverted ones who'll do anything to anyone. Seriously, there are rules ... [points emphatically at his chest] ... I have rules.

Kevin's frustration is understandable given that cultural norms script successful relationships in terms of dual sexual and emotional exclusivity, and any alternative to that is rendered promiscuous, different, subpar, low status, impossible, or even wrong. The dual stigma of being bisexual and nonmonogamous can be taxing when simply discussing, let alone experiencing, multiple partners because of such social disapproval.

Clarice, a twenty-one-year-old heterosexual woman, related that she and her boyfriend, Mariz, had placed limitations on the kind of sex they had with others:

> **Clarice:** So, like, Mariz can have oral with someone else. I don't care so much about that. And he's fine, too, like if I wanna have oral sex with another guy.
> **Interviewer:** What about vaginal penetration?
> **Clarice:** Oh, yeah, sure. Yeah, yeah. That's fine, too. Just not anal. Mariz is weird about it ... he wants to keep the whole anal thing

between us. I think it's 'cause he worked so long to get me to do it that if I just have it with another guy he feels like I'm giving it away too easily, you know?

Abbey, Kevin, and Clarice, like nearly all the nonmonogamous intervie-wees, had rules that governed sexual behaviors with others. The most common rules prohibited certain kinds of sexual penetration, such as vaginal or anal sex. Although there were few differences between men and women with regard to establishing different rules about behaviors, sexual orientation proved to be a factor. Among heterosexual men and women, oral sex was the least regulated; vaginal penetration was also little regulated. Bisexuals had the fewest overall restrictions on sexual behavior, although bisexual men had rules similar to those of gay men. Gay men indicated a number of restrictions governing anal penetration, as Roger did: "I can do whatever I want with other guys, just not anal sex. That's what we do together. Plus, it's safer that way because of what's out there. It's harder to contract something doing just oral or jacking off."

Overall, rules about sexual behavior centered on safety and on restricting certain types of sexual interaction with other partners. Estab-lishing these rules about safety, different kinds of sex acts, locations for sex, times of day, and the absence of kids serves several purposes. First, simply having rules denotes that some level of responsibility, respect, and expectation is placed on partners, operating like traditional sexual fidelity. Second, restricting certain types of activity preserves a pair bond between partners, as in Kevin and Christine's case, in which she wanted Kevin to share oral sex with only her. Clarice's rule about anal sex with her boyfriend also demonstrates that some prefer to keep certain activ-ities between primary partners only not because of safety concerns but rather because a feeling of specialness is attached to the behavior.

Rules that Designate Other Partners

Many nonmonogamists also had rules about who could be a possible partner based on attributes, such as gender, age, race, or connection to the individuals. This is a common rule category that exemplifies the way most nonmonogamous relationships are constructed. Sometimes the rules had been immediately established, and others had been introduced as the relationship's nonmonogamy evolved:

> I'm fine if she has sex with another girl, but not a guy.
> —Peter, 23, heterosexual

> We have one rule about others: no coworkers or mutual friends.
> —Jacob, 37, gay

> I didn't want her to be younger than me.
> —Karen, 32, heterosexual

> Our rule is that we can hook up but they can't be from [city]. Only if we go out of town or it's not someone from around here.
> —Alex, 45, gay

> I have this thing about my body. I am really self-conscious about my ass. So if there is a girl, like for instance a black girl, and she has a bigger ass than me, then I get upset. So I prefer that Tommy doesn't hook up with black girls even though he's black, 'cause, well, you know, I have no ass and they do. Unless she has no ass [laughs], then he can ask me and maybe I'll okay it.
> —Sara, 26, bisexual

Peter's rule about restricting his girlfriend (who is bisexual) from having sex with other men but not women was echoed by several bisexuals in this study. Others (Klesse 2006; McLean 2004) found this particular restriction common in bisexual relationships, a phenomenon occasionally referred to as *gender monogamy*. More heterosexual women were restricted by their partners from having sex with other men, and several bisexual women were encouraged by their male partners to be with other women, sometimes in a group-sex situation. Gendered restrictions privilege male sexual desire and restrict women's pleasure through heteronormative, masculinist ideals. This occurs most often through encouraging female same-sex eroticism as a component of male sexual fantasies while restricting women from exploring or fulfilling their own sexual desires, as Sara noted:

> When we were first married, I was scared to tell him I was bisexual. I waited a while actually, and then it just came out one day. We talked about having threesomes and how he could watch and eventually participate. When I told him I wanted to have a threesome with him and another guy, well, the shit totally hit the fan. He freaked out, and I was so pissed off. Why is it okay for him to have a threesome with two girls but it's not okay for me to have one with two guys?

Another interviewee, Barbara, described the way her boyfriend resisted her involvement with other women unless he was there to "benefit":

> I was going to this support group and met a woman who was also bisexual and had a boyfriend. She was so beautiful, you know? I told Fletcher that I wanted to see her, and he said he wanted to meet her first and then maybe we could have a threesome together if he approves. Well, we all ended up at the bar together one night. We went back to our apartment, and the next thing you know I'm on the floor giving him a blow job and *she's* kneeling next to me giving her boyfriend a blow job. I remember looking up and seeing Fletcher and Max high-five each other [pauses, continues with voice elevated]—high-fiving each other while we gave them head. I felt like such a slut; you know, like I was a dirty whore. I just feel like he was the one who benefited, not me. I wanted to be with her first, you know.

Sara's and Barbara's experiences highlight that even when women engage sexual agency and attempt to fulfill their sexual desires through nonmonogamy, their male partners resort to restrictions that allow themselves rather than their female partners to benefit. Swinging literature confirms this pattern in terms of women who are initially encouraged to participate in swinging and are subsequently discouraged by their male partners because they "enjoy it too much" (see Paulson and Paulson 1970).

Jacob and Alex are representative of several who disallowed mutual friends, past lovers, coworkers, and locals as possible partners. More specific limitations, like those of Karen and Sara, seem rather arbitrary but are in fact representative of personal preferences, insecurities, and concerns that nonmonogamous individuals commonly regulate through various rules, boundaries, and limitations.

Establishing rules about other partners occasionally included "veto power," which allows partners to disapprove of specific individuals as potential partners. Martin, a twenty-nine-year-old heterosexual swinger, described how veto power worked in his relationship; I followed up by asking if he had ever exercised veto power:

> We have veto power with each other. If there's a guy that Hannah wants to have sex with, I get to say yea or nay. She has the same power with me ... The last time I used veto power was with this guy at a sex club. I just didn't like his vibe, you know? He was all over Hannah, and I could tell he used [drugs]. So I said no way, and she was cool with it. We've never had problems with not agreeing with each other's vetoes.

Several interviewees described veto power as an extension of the basic rules upon which they had agreed and said that it was usually invoked in particular circumstances, such as unsafe contexts and specific individuals. Others described this as "the final say" rather than veto power, denoting a permission-based system that varied according to time, place, and behavior.

Rules about Disclosure

A common interviewee theme centered on disclosing one's interest in a potential partner, an upcoming date, or details about a successful encounter. Being up front, open, and honest about multiple partners is a cornerstone and, for some, an added benefit of consensual nonmonogamy. Some considered disclosure a necessity, whereas others preferred to not know times, dates, or details. Rules about not knowing what one's partner is doing, will do, or has done with another have been cited in other studies, particularly on gay male couples (Ramirez and Brown 2010).

Nonmonogamists in this study, regardless of sexual orientation, were more likely to prefer a "don't ask, don't tell" policy than polyamorists were. However, almost all interviewees discussed establishing rules about disclosure at various degrees. For example, David, a forty-two-year-old gay man involved with his boyfriend, Rico, described their initial disclosure rules:

> I—well, we wanted to have full disclosure so that we wouldn't be embarrassed, like if we were at a party and some guy comes up and says, "Hey, I fucked your boyfriend," you know? So I need to know.

In addition to preventing embarrassment, full disclosure provided an avenue for sexual excitement. Genevieve, a twenty-one-year-old bisexual woman married to a heterosexual man, commented, "I don't need to know before something happens, but I want to know after. Actually, it's kinda hot when he tells me." Roger, a twenty-three-year-old gay man, described the way he and his boyfriend, Brach, exchange details of their extradyadic sexual encounters:

> Sometimes I can't wait to hear about Brach's evenings. I ask him to tell me when we're in bed, and then I take off his shirt while he describes him, what they did, and how turned on he was. It gets me excited just hearing about it (I can't believe I'm telling you this—he'd kill me). Just last night, we were—well, we were in the throes of passion, and he described one of his most recent evenings ... and while he was telling me I came so hard [laughs], I could have been sixteen again!

Like David and Genevieve, many interviewees described disclosure as comforting—and as assurance that they could talk about other partners—whether the reason behind it was to avoid embarrassment, become aroused, or simply know. Disclosure remains an important concept in nonmonogamy, especially because secret sexual encounters are fairly common in monogamous relationships. The ability to be open about multiple sexual encounters was discussed as liberating for most; however, some experienced difficulty with the total-honesty approach:

> Fletcher and I can tell each other anything about what happens, but I dunno. I just find myself having a hard time telling him what I do with other women. He is so supportive, and it's not like he's getting off on it, but I guess it's just hard to describe the connection that happens between two women.
>
> —Barbara, 36, bisexual

> I like that we can be totally open, but I usually don't tell her a hundred percent of the details. I feel like she would freak out if she knew exactly what I did. No—not like that 'cause I can do whatever I want. I, um, I guess it's like I want to protect her in a way. Like I worry she'll be hurt if there's something she doesn't like.
>
> —Daniel, 24, heterosexual

Whereas agreements like Daniel's and that between Fletcher and Barbara encourage full disclosure (even if it is not practiced), some interviewees had chosen to establish a less explicit agreement. Oden, a thirty-five-year-old heterosexual man, had been dating his girlfriend of several years, Tina Marie: "We have a don't ask, don't tell policy. I don't want to know, and she doesn't either. And I really don't want her to tell me." A few commented that they had yet to establish formal rules of disclosure—some because their nonmonogamy was a recent development, and others because they simply had never got around to making official rules. One interviewee relayed that in the thirty years he and his partner had been together, they had not divulged their lovers nor attempted to have a conversation about disclosure. Upon completion of the interview, he commented that he was going home to talk with his partner about their lack of rules and to set up a formal agreement—and thanked me for the insight.

Among interviewees, rules about behavior, other partners, and disclosure had often been established and renegotiated through "the talk" or a similar conversation to solidify formal agreements like those described by survey respondents. Self-imposed rules, however, surfaced during the interviews as a category not originally anticipated in the survey design.

Self-Imposed Rules as a Distinct Category of Regulation

A separate category of rules emerged with several experienced nonmonogamists. Self-imposed rules comprise rules, boundaries, or limitations that originate individually, without consultation with one's partner(s). This is an important distinction because the motivation or intent of self-imposed rules rests upon the notion of rule making not between partners but rather solely by the individual. For example, William, a thirty-three-year-old bisexual man casually dating several men and women, said, "I make it a rule that I never participate in deception—if he/she has a boyfriend or girlfriend who expects monogamy, then I am not going to help violate that." William's commitment to honesty originated and was adhered to not because a partner requested it; he did not create the rule ultimately for another's benefit—rather, he had imposed the rule upon himself. Whereas some rules, like those governing safe sex and disclosure, can be both mutually and self-imposed, others remained in the distinct self-imposed category. For example, Marilyn, a twenty-seven-year-old heterosexual woman, described several rules that she had made for herself:

> I never double book. And I always leave Saturday nights open for my husband. It's not in our agreement, but I just want to have some time set aside for spontaneity. Even if we don't end up doing anything together, I'll still leave it open out of respect for him and, well, us.

Similarly, Timothy, a twenty-two-year-old gay man dating several partners, described his "one and only" self-imposed rule, which he referred to as his "twenty-four-hour rule":

> I have this thing about not fucking two different partners in the
> same day—like a twenty-four-hour rule. Group stuff doesn't count
> [laughs], you know, but, like, if I hook-up with Julio in the after-
> noon and then see Remy later that day, I won't have sex with
> Remy. Even if I take a shower and I'm all clean. I guess I feel like
> I owe each of them some respect!

Nancy's comment about double booking and Timothy's twenty-four-
hour rule echo what Atwater (1982) described as "time norms." Her study
on women engaged in extramarital relations finds that half of her sample
had had sex on the same day with both husband and lover, reporting
difficulty in handling the experience. Atwater discussed this difficulty in
terms of needing sufficient time between partners in order to "insulate
them from the effect of competing social and sexual situations" (Atwater
1982, 130–132).[1] Having enough time between sexual partners serves to
cognitively, physically, and emotionally distinguish partners, even for
those engaged in consensual nonmonogamy.

The significance of self-imposed rules is most apparent when
assessing how nonmonogamy is constructed. Because rules are discussed
between partners, a certain level of commitment is necessary to follow
the rules or at least acknowledge that they have been established. Who
is held accountable when one violates his or her self-imposed rules?
Further, what purpose do self-imposed rules serve in negotiating guilt,
perpetuating disclosure, and differentiating between emotional and
sexual fidelity? Self-imposed rules contribute a layer to nonmonogamy
that has not formerly been addressed.

Rule Functions: Feeling Special through Specified Fidelity

In examining rules that govern behavior, other partners, and disclosure,
one must acknowledge the relevance of establishing and maintaining
such rules. Though the basic purpose of the rules seems to be protecting

the body from harm (i.e., safe sex), rules also work to minimize jealousy, maintain boundaries, and signify a certain level of commitment and respect for a partner's wishes. A common pattern emerged wherein the rules indicate a regulated resistance to sexual exclusivity while simultaneously demonstrating an embracement of emotional exclusivity. This often surfaced in the form of feeling special. Feeling special is ultimately achieved through specified fidelity, which denotes the importance of remaining emotionally committed to each other while negotiating (and often regulating) multiple sexual interactions.

Katie, a thirty-two-year-old heterosexual woman, had been married to Todd for over eight years. About two years into the relationship, they decided to be nonmonogamous and established several rules about their newly opened relationship. Their agreement highlights the way that specified fidelity ensures specialness between the two: "I didn't want him to spend the night at someone else's place. We also never had sex in our bed with other people unless we were together. And absolutely, without question, we cannot fall in love with anyone else." Interviewees like Katie discussed falling in love as the most prohibited interaction with extradyadic partners, a restriction that preserves emotional exclusivity. Clay, a nineteen-year-old heterosexual man dating his girlfriend of several months, described his current arrangement as "totally not restrictive" but involving specified fidelity: "My girlfriend told me that I can do whatever; just don't fall in love."

Both Katie and Clay had agreements of a type fairly common among the interviewees. In terms of gender, women and men were both likely to restrict falling in love with extradyadic partners. Whereas cultural norms suggest that women are more emotional and men are more sexual, gender was not a predictor of limiting sexual or emotional interactions in order to preserve feeling special. Sexual orientation also proved to be less distinct than expected. Again, gay and bisexual men have, perhaps, the most experience with nonmonogamous relationships that rely on rules, boundaries, and limitations (Blumstein and Schwartz 1983; Harry

1984; Laumann et al. 1994; Green 2006). The gay and bisexual men in this study confirm that nonmonogamy remains a common relationship structure; however, relatively few of their rules differed from those of other orientations, especially in regard to falling in love with others.

Jamison, a twenty-three-year-old bisexual man, asserted that safe-sex rules, specific to potentially HIV-positive partners, were most important. However, Jamison also commented on the rule of emotional exclusivity through specified fidelity with his boyfriend, alluding once again to specialness: "He can have sex with anyone, but we keep the love between us. That's our way of being special, I guess. It's different than hooking up because that's just sex. It's special ... because *we're* in love." Because Jamison, like many bisexual and gay men, had several sexual partners, negotiating intimacy and connectedness with his primary partner remained a concern. Feeling or being special was the most common way interviewees articulated such a need.

David (previously introduced) recounted that he and his boyfriend, Rico, often engaged in a competition at the local gay bar to obtain numbers and potential hookups. Their rules about safe sex, no colleagues or friends, and full disclosure were typical, but David spent considerable time struggling with jealousy and the need to feel special:

> Every man I know would love to have ten people totally monogamous to him but allow him to fuck anybody. When I get that twinge like maybe Rico is fucking around, I have to remember that I was sucking some guy off last week! I guess I just want to know that I'm number one. Even if there are other guys, *I'm* his boyfriend. *I'm* special.

David represents a number of study participants who, though they exhibited a sexually nontraditional approach to relationships, still operated under the constraints of dyadic design and emotional exclusivity. David's concern about Rico's "fucking around" seems surprising given that their relationship had been and remained sexually nonmonogamous. Several interviewees touched upon this paradox of practicing nonmonogamy in a mononormative society, describing it best as "I can do it, but it bothers me if he/she does it." This is demonstrated by survey data from nonmonogamists, polyamorists, and even some monogamists: respondents indicated *being allowed* to engage in extradyadic behaviors at a greater percentage than they indicated that they *allowed* their primary partners to engage in similar behaviors with others.

Further, the rules that Katie, Clay, Jamison, and David had clearly allow sexual relations with others but restrict emotional (or love) interactions. Such a distinction between emotional and sexual exclusivity occurred in both the kinds of rules and the terms interviewees used to describe their nonmonogamous relationships. Again, this exemplifies the importance of specified fidelity in preserving commitment and specialness between partners while allowing for multiple sexual partners.

For one couple in particular, the process of establishing the rules of nonmonogamy, negotiating them, and justifying the purpose of differentiating sexual and emotional exclusivity (thus, specified fidelity) is most representative. Diane and Gary demonstrate the negotiation of rules and boundaries while contextualizing their concerns about preserving emotional intimacy through specified fidelity. Diane and Gary, both fifty-two, Jewish, and heterosexual, had been together for three and a half years and had been married for three months. Although Gary was the primary interviewee, after our initial conversation, he requested that Diane be included in the interview. Diane soon joined us on a separate phone in another part of their home, resulting in a candid three-hour interview with them both.[2] I began by asking one question of Gary and later weaving in a similar question for Diane, or vice versa. As the interview progressed, it became more of a three-way conversation. I asked Diane to describe their relationship in terms of whether they were monogamous or nonmonogamous, and she responded, "I wouldn't want Gary to share his heart with somebody else. But if he wants to rub genitals with somebody else, that's fine by me." Diane's description denotes a derogation of sex and reduces such contact to bodily function, deepening the separation between sexual and emotional involvement. Diane and Gary later stated that they were sexually nonmonogamous together, at weekend retreats, at BDSM (bondage, dominance/discipline, sadism, masochism) clubs, and at private gatherings. They did not have separate partners, nor did they wish to have distinct experiences. Both described enjoying "playing" together with others in the form of erotic massage, teasing, and sensuous touching. When I asked about any agreements or rules they had about their play, the following exchange occurred:

> **Gary:** We try to set our boundaries and our limits ahead of time so there isn't any confusion. And one of the things that's really great about Diane is that we communicate, I think, pretty effectively with each other.
> **Interviewer:** What are the boundaries or limits you set ahead of time?
> **Diane:** Well, I won't let—I don't want other partners to play with me. I don't want other partners to touch me; I'm just not into— I'm just not into other partners. Um, so, when we do meet another partner, you know, we'll tell them that, you know, we want you to play with me, with Gary, but I'm not interested in having them play with me.
> **Gary:** Which is always a problem because Diane is a pretty hot and a desirable partner and everybody wants to play with her (laughter in unison).
> **Diane:** And, um, what else do we say? No intercourse.
> **Gary:** No, what is it, no penile penetration?
> **Diane:** Yeah, no penile penetration. Um, what other boundaries do we have, Gary?
> **Gary:** Ah, let's see. Well, we're not into paying people, either [laughs]. We do safe, sane, and consensual.

Diane and Gary's conversation reveals that they knew, understood, and agreed on the rules, and although they did not identify specifics about falling in love, they disagreed on the emotional significance of certain activities:

Diane: I don't want to share his heart with anybody. I really don't. Interestingly enough, I don't want to say it's off limits, but I have a hard time if I see Gary kissing someone because that to me is much more intimate than if I see someone rubbing genitals or even oral–genital sex.

Gary: I don't completely agree. To me, kissing isn't the same as it is to Diane. I agree with her completely that I have no desire to share my heart with anyone else. I am totally, hopelessly, completely in love with Diane and uh, I'm happy as a pig in shit that way. But that does not extend—I mean, I separate sex from love.

Diane: He does much more so than I do. And that's why I still have an issue with that because it's hard for me to see you [Gary, on the phone in a separate room] kissing another woman and thinking there's no emotion going on there because it's hard for me to do that. [Addressing interviewer:] So Gary is much more capable of separating sex from love than me, at this point.

Gary: The emotion that I'm kissing them with is because I want to uh, have sex with them, but I don't want to go home with them. I want to go home with you.

Because Gary and Diane identified as "emotionally monogamous," I asked why preserving emotional fidelity was so important:

Diane: It's so special; it's so unique to Gary and me. I guess it's just a very fulfilling feeling knowing that you love somebody more than anything in the whole world and knowing that that feeling is completely and fully reciprocated; it is just about the most special, warmest, safest, comforting, delicious feeling. To me, it's better than sex, and I love sex ... And you know what's interesting? I don't think I've ever been in a relationship with anybody before Gary [in which] I would have been comfortable with him being with other partners because I am so secure in the emotional bond that we have, and I've never had that with anybody else—which makes it so special. I mean, I never thought I'd be capable and the only reason why I feel I'm capable is because of the emotional commitment we have for one another.

For Diane, specified fidelity via emotional exclusivity ensured special-ness through reciprocity, safety, and comfort. However, her comment also unearths a final consideration regarding the importance of specified fidelity: when dyads retain emotional exclusivity, this can operate as the central enabler to sexual nonmonogamy. In other words, when the rela-tionship is emotionally preserved, multiple sexual encounters serve as a bonus or addition rather than a substitution for inadequacies or unmet needs.

Different types of nonmonogamy require a range of rules that govern behavior and establish boundaries between partners. Some intervie-wees discussed rules for engaging separate extradyadic partners, and others discussed agreements for participating in situations where both primary partners were present (e.g., Gary and Diane). Some described attending sex parties with their partner(s) and had specific rules for playing together with others at the parties. Permission was a key compo-nent of such rules. I spoke extensively with Melanie, a thirty-three-year-old woman who had been married to her husband, Owen, for eight years. They had begun swinging about five years earlier and regularly hosted and attended sex parties in their community. Melanie was candid about their struggles with rule negotiations, feeling special, and ensuring spec-ified fidelity throughout the interview. She spoke of obtaining permis-sion from one another during a party as important but said that it was sometimes difficult to adhere to this rule. She relayed the following about her most recent sex party adventure with Owen:

> **Melanie:** Our last party we went to was about a month ago. There was this unicorn [a first-time sex party attendee] who totally captivated us. I mean she was *hot*. Owen was all over her right away. So I started to touch her breasts, you know, while Owen was making drinks and she was into it, so he was ready to go. And I was like—I wasn't even sure she was okay with it because I think she was a friend of the host or something. But she touched my breasts too and we started to kiss and it was so hot because it was right there. I mean, I love it when people watch, and it was

right there in the living room. So Owen takes her hand and mine and takes us to one of the bedrooms, so she could have more, you know, more privacy. And she was so much fun [giggles]. She was really cool about pleasing me first, and Owen watched, and then kept asking if it was okay that she had Owen's cock in her mouth. And we kept asking her if it was okay too that we were basically all having sex and it was, you know, it was consensual. After she came, she wanted me and Owen to have sex while she watched. She was like perfect because we played together but she also recognized that Owen and I needed our special time.

Interviewer: Why is it important for you and Owen have special time at a sex party?

Melanie: Well, it's like we need to connect to make sure we're on the same page, you know? There are all these people fucking around you, some you know, and some are new, and it's a chance to connect and reassure one another that you're the priority. And that you're honoring one another.

Interviewer: What do you mean by "honoring one another"?

Melanie: Following our rules, you know? Owen has a really high sex drive, and I like playing with women. So we have rules about what we can and can't do at parties, because to be honest with you, sometimes it—it kind of bothers me if he goes off and does his own thing with me not there. These parties are a chance for us to play together. For him to get his needs met and for me to, you know, play with girls. We were at a party and he went off with another girl and didn't ask permission first. I flipped out and was really mad. I was like, seriously? This isn't so you can go and fuck whoever. It's so we can experience it *together*.

Interviewer: What are the rules you have?

Melanie: Well, we need to ask each other's permission if we want to play with someone alone. And we always use condoms. Except with one another. I'm on birth control. And nothing goes in his ass. Ever! But my ass is fair game [laughs]. They're pretty basic. I think a lot of couples have these rules.

Interviewer: What happens if one of you breaks the rules?

Melanie: Um... [laughs]. honestly, not much. Let's just say he breaks them more than I do. Maybe it's just because he's a guy and he can't control himself. Like I said, he's got a really high sex drive. At the last party, actually—that unicorn we met—I mean, I liked her so it wasn't a big deal, but after we all played together, she wanted to fuck again. So he came and asked for my permission, like he was supposed to ... I was really tired and passed out in one of the bedrooms, and when I woke up, I went to find him. Turns out he was in another room fucking her again. I got kind of pissed because he was supposed to ask my permission. I don't know, maybe he thought since I was okay with it the first time, he could do it again. I felt like he kind of snuck away while I was asleep, you know?

Interviewer: Did you confront him?

Melanie: Yeah, but nothing really came of it. He told me he was trying to give her a good time, since it was her first time and all. He'd probably be pissed if I did the same thing, but I don't know, actually. That's a good point, actually [laughs]. I don't think I've ever not asked permission.

Melanie's account highlights a fairly typical scenario at a sex party, which is a contemporary version of the swinging parties customary in the 1960s and 1970s. Sex parties are usually held in a private home or hotel suite and vary in terms of who can attend and which behaviors are acceptable during the event. Most parties encourage heterosexual couples' attendance, and single women are always allowed, though single male attendees are less common. Notably, there are well-established general rules for the parties, involving a minimum age and encouraged and prohibited conduct, such as "no" means no, condoms required unless otherwise requested, no touching unless invited, no exchanging money for sex acts, respect boundaries, clean up after oneself, and keep pleasure as the focus.

Gendered dynamics and boundary negotiations are important aspects of swinging and can illuminate the preservation of significance and feeling special for those involved. Many of today's sex parties still perpetuate normative masculinity, male homophobia, and a more illusionary form of female sexual agency, as with Melanie's recent experience. Further, although agreements and boundaries are often set between couples before a party begins, they are continually negotiated once the party has started and are sometimes broken or violated before the party has finished. The rules, once again, ensure specialness or significance in some capacity between partners.

Interview and survey data in unison demonstrate that nonmonogamists expend considerable effort encouraging sexual multiplicities while preserving emotional exclusivity through rules, boundaries, and limitations. The result is specified fidelity that ensures one's feeling special because the rules are carefully established based on partners' needs and subsequently followed through commitment to the rules —and therefore to the relationship. Perhaps the notion of feeling special also serves to reduce jealousy between partners. If one feels special, primary, or "number one," this reduces the need to be jealous of the time, attention, and interactions one's partner has with others.

The rules of nonmonogamy could be an extension of Struening's (2002) concept of a *new intimacy* that allows people to define their relationships in their own ways. The "new intimacy deal" that characterizes love relationships post-1960 suggests that decisions should not be controlled by external expectations or social conventions (Struening 2002, 14). Though there is a pretense or conceit of agency within this notion, at the same time the model is heavily scripted. Consciously making rules that allow sexual interactions with multiple partners places consensual nonmonogamy at the forefront of contemporary intimate relationships. However, nonmonogamy can have an almost compulsory quality, both in design and practice, that circumvents individual agency. For instance, nonmonogamy has become normalized within gay male and many bisexual circles, resulting in more awareness about established agreements and similar rules and regulations. It also positions those who choose monogamy as the exception. If people are heavily channeled into relationship models by their gender and sexual orientations, then Struening's idea of self-determination in romantic relationships is illusory.

Further, by restricting multiple *emotional* partners, nonmonogamous individuals find themselves positioned squarely within the ideal of a new intimacy paradigm that relies on the master template of dyadic monogamy. And although Shumway (2003) acknowledged that intimacy may manifest in sexual relations *and or* emotional closeness, data from this study confirm that great weight continues to be attributed to emotional intimacy (see Struening 2002).

Nonmonogamists often invoked the rules in describing their relationships as committed or in stating that they had committed to the relationship by creating rules and subsequently following them. Given that *commitment* is a term utilized in monogamous relationships, in part because it conveys dual fidelity, it is interesting that so many nonmonogamists discussed commitment. This could be correlated with general cultural trends that encourage new terminologies of commitment and intimacy in discussing contemporary relationships, or it could be a deliberate attempt to legitimize nonmonogamy through mononormative language.

Shumway is quick to point out that intimacy, the goal of most love relationships, does not always arrive with commitment (2003, 143). I argue that commitment does not always arrive with monogamy, especially in a diverse, contemporary society. In constructing their relationships, nonmonogamous individuals embrace notions of intimacy and commitment but nuance them through their approaches to multiple sexual partners. They somewhat reify, however, the importance of relational intimacy by restricting multiple loves and keeping emotional exclusivity in order to remain loyal and feel special. Commitment therefore transpires through specified fidelity as individuals make rules and agreements about sexual, nonsexual, and emotional interactions with multiple partners. Commitment also occurs when individuals follow the rules, and for some, specified fidelity extends from renegotiating the rules when they are not followed.

Violations and Renegotiations: Breaking the Rules of Nonmonogamy

In discussing how nonmonogamy is structured and practiced, the inevitable question arises, what happens if (or when) the rules are broken? In traditional monogamous relationships, violating the rules of fidelity carries severe consequences that often include divorce, separation, or breaking up. In such relationships, expectations of dual fidelity are occasionally articulated, but the penalties of failing those expectations are also cemented, as in one monogamous respondent's comment: "If he ever cheats on me, I'll kill him!"

I asked nonmonogamists if they had ever violated or broken the rules and what had happened as a result. Some responded that because there were agreed-upon rules, cheating was not really an issue for them; it is not possible. Georgia, a sixty-year-old bisexual woman active in several alternative-lifestyle communities, emphatically stated, "Cheating is for monogamy! I don't cheat because I am in an open relationship and my husband gives me permission to be with my girlfriend. I am open with him—that is certainly not cheating." Survey data show, however, that nonmonogamous individuals report higher rates of cheating on a partner (30%) than monogamous individuals (21%; table 7). This is an unexpected finding given Georgia's comment, which represents the attitude of many nonmonogamous survey respondents and interviewees.

Table 7. Survey respondents' reported rates of cheating by monogamists and nonmonogamists.

Have You Cheated on Your Current Partner?

	Monogamous N=1363	Nonmonogamous N=512
Yes	22%	38%
No	78	61
Refused to Answer	*	*

Has Your Current Partner Cheated on You?

	Monogamous N=1363	Nonmonogamous N=512
Yes	9%	27%
No	90	70
Refused to Answer	*	2

*Less than 1%

Although monogamists probably underreport rates of cheating, one may assume that nonmonogamous individuals overreport incidents of cheating, responding that they cheat according to a mononormative definition of cheating: having sexual relations with someone else. These results are confirmed through two additional patterns in both survey and interview data.

First, examining data from those nonmonogamous survey respondents who indicated that they allowed or were allowed to engage in activities with others shows that 39% had been involved in behavior with others that was not allowed. Further, 29% also reported that their primary partner had engaged in unallowed behavior with others. These results are consistent with nonmonogamists' reported rates of cheating in this study (figure 7).

Figure 7. Nonmonogamous survey respondents' cheating rates compared to engagement in unallowed behaviors with others.

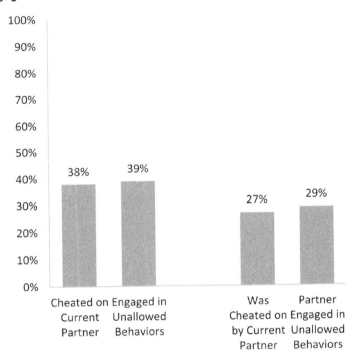

Second, interview data indicate that the concept of cheating does in fact remain salient among nonmonogamous relationships. Margie, a thirty-eight-year old woman who had recently begun a primary relationship with a heterosexual man and his wife, commented,

> I'm glad we're talking about this because I think cheating does occur in nonmonogamous relationships, but no one likes to talk

about it. We all think that because we can have sex with other people that cheating doesn't exist. But it does; I've cheated, I've been cheated on, and I have broken the rules many times. Just because we aren't exclusive and we have rules doesn't mean that we *follow* every rule.

Jorge, a thirty-nine-year-old bisexual man recently divorced from his wife and at the time of the interview involved with an "older gentleman," offered his perspective on how nonmonogamy can be conceived as an applied reaction to cheating:

> When I was married to my wife, I began an Internet relationship with a man that I ended up meeting in person. I didn't plan on having sex with him because I love my wife ... but I eventually did with him. She found out while she was looking through my e-mails. She was so, so upset—I couldn't bear the thought of hurting Lois, and so I let her decide what she wanted to do. She actually came up with the idea of opening our marriage. I—well, we had a talk about my sexuality, and then a few months later she suggested it. She didn't act on it at first, hoping I would just get the bisexuality stuff out of my system. But I had a number of male sex partners.

Jorge's situation presents an alternative explanation of why rates of cheating among the nonmonogamous survey sample are much higher than expected. If there has been cheating at some point in the relationship, as with Jorge, a decision is made to be nonmonogamous in order to allow for consensual, rather than secretive, extradyadic connections. This pattern may be more widespread than it appears in reported data.

Table 8. Nonmonogamous survey respondents' cheating rates by gender and sexual orientation.

Have You Cheated on Your Current Partner?

	N	Yes	No
Total Women	200	36%	64%
Lesbian Women	17	41%	59%
Bisexual Women	81	25	75
Straight Women	93	44	56
Total Men	305	23%	77%
Gay Men	99	44%	56%
Bisexual Men	42	45	55
Straight Men	155	36	54

*Has Your Current Partner Cheated on You?^*

	N	Yes	No
Total Women	192	38%	62%
Lesbian Women	17	18%	82%
Bisexual Women	79	24	76
Straight Women	88	25	75
Total Men	297	30%	70%
Gay Men	95	40%	60%
Bisexual Men	42	21	79
Straight Men	151	26	74

Note: Queer/Other respondents were less than 1%
^Several respondents (less than 1%) refused to answer

There were few statistically significant relationships between gender, sexual orientation, and rates of cheating among nonmonogamists. In the distribution of cheating across sexual orientation, nonmonogamous bisexual women had the lowest rates of cheating, whereas nonmonogamous gay and bisexual men had the highest rates of cheating. Heterosexual women also reported higher rates of cheating than their male counterparts, with an 8% difference (table 8).

In attempting to explain such high rates of cheating, or rule violation, among nonmonogamists, perhaps there was some confusion in terms of respondents' assuming that the researcher's (that is, my) definition of cheating involved any sort of extradyadic behavior, rather than reporting such involvement based on their own definitions of cheating or breaking the rules. However, interview data resolved this concern, further illustrating the reality that many nonmonogamists do, in fact, cheat.

When encouraged to use their own definitions of cheating, a number of interviewees admitted to having cheated on their current partners. This study finds that nonmonogamous individuals unintentionally and deliberately define cheating in terms that resist mononormativity, referring to such activity as breaking the rules. Further, what constitutes breaking the rules is not confined to sexual activity. However, the act of secretively or deliberately violating agreements remains salient, even for nonmonogamists. Heather, a twenty-nine-year-old bisexual woman involved with four partners, was asked to define cheating. She responded, "Cheating is breaking the rules. Any kind of rule we've established in my relationships is there for a reason. If I break one of those rules, I'm cheating. Otherwise, how can you trust your partners, you know?" I asked Heather if she ever broke the rules, to which she replied, "Let's just say that nobody's perfect." Abbey (previously introduced) discussed what happened when she broke the rules that her boyfriend's wife had established:

> You know how we weren't supposed to do anything in their bed, right? Well, one time we were wrestling and ended up doing some

oral sex on their bed. I'm not sure if he fessed up to his wife, but I considered it cheating; we broke the rules. And I know the rule came into existence because he had had sex with someone else in their bed without checking first.

Some interviewees said that certain behaviors could "technically" be considered cheating but found justification for engaging in the behavior. Casey, a twenty-two-year-old heterosexual woman in a serious relationship with her boyfriend of three years, Mark, said that she and Mark were moving to a different state at the time of the interview. Mark had already moved to their new home, and Casey had stayed behind to pack the final boxes and help the movers finish the transition:

> Our rule was no sex with others in our bed. Well, Mark had already moved and it was just me in our apartment for the last night. I had someone over, and we ended up having sex on our bed. *But*, I knew I was going to throw it out since we had a new bed at the new house, so it technically wasn't our bed anymore. Technically.

Casey's example acknowledges a less concrete subtext of agreements and violations. In nonmonogamy, the ideal notion of agreeing on rules and subsequently following them is, of course, easier said than done. Partners disagree on allowing certain behaviors, potential partners, and levels of disclosure. Even self-imposed rules have room for flexibility and fluctuate depending on circumstances. The goal of renegotiation is to acknowledge what works and what needs improvement while attempting nonmonogamy. Within the discussion of rule making and rule breaking, there exists a gray zone, a question whether something "really counts."

One case in particular exemplifies the struggle for successful nonmonogamy within this gray zone. Paul, a twenty-five-year-old bisexual-gay man, and his partner, Joe, a twenty-seven-year-old gay man, had struggled with closing and opening their relationship of three years, surviving multiple incidents of cheating, rule violations, and renegotiations. At the beginning of the interview, Paul explained the status of the relationship:

> Right now we're open, but only for hookups and casual sex. I consider us to be monogamous in terms of emotion—he's my boyfriend, and I love him, and he loves me. But commitment is like a straightjacket to me, and I am just not satisfied with him sexually. That's why I like the open part.

Paul discussed the rules that the pair had established together about safe sex, no anal penetration, and full disclosure and that had remained salient throughout the previous three years, acknowledging that he had broken each rule on several occasions, as had Joe. Paul described the most recent situation, which had occurred several days before the interview:

> I just hooked up with this guy the other week. He was so hot—and, well, we fucked. I just couldn't bring myself to tell Joe. Things have been going so well that I just didn't want to mess it up. I guess when it comes down to it, I'm gonna do whatever I need to do be satisfied, even if it means, you know, breaking the rules.

Although Paul both had helped establish and had subsequently agreed to follow the rules, he was not completely satisfied with them, intensifying the possibility of his violating them and potentially affecting the renegotiation process. Paul and Joe had made several attempts to allow for more flexibility with outside partners, although few rules had been successfully followed. Throughout their relationship, Paul and Joe also struggled with the benefits of multiple sexual partners and the unexpected negative effect on their emotional bond. After describing this recent hookup, Paul talked extensively about how well things had been going with Joe until he found out that Joe had broken the rules:

> I looked in his phone and saw text messages from this other guy that said, "Hey, wanna cum fuck me tonight?" Shit like that. I flipped. I couldn't believe he was doing it again behind my back, even though we agreed this time we'd tell each other.

Though the rules work best when people follow them, like Paul, many interviewees articulated their struggles with adhering to even the most basic rules. If rules allow such a wide range of behavior with multiple partners, why do people continue to break them? The data in this study cannot answer such an inquiry, but based on Paul's story, one could imagine a continuous struggle between what individuals want, what they get, and which contextual factors prohibit them from fulfilling their needs under circumstances that present few alternatives to the master relationship template. In addition, there could also be an ambivalence about wanting intimacy on a more personal level—the notion of longing for connectedness yet being afraid of having it or wanting to have it with another person. When I asked Paul if he ever felt bad or guilty about breaking the rules, he replied,

> Most of the time, not really. But I've noticed that the times I feel most guilty are when I get close to someone, spend time with them. Like the guy I fucked the other night—it was weird because I woke up the next morning with this horrible sense of guilt. Like I almost didn't go into work because I felt so guilty. I think I felt so bad because I ended up hanging out with the guy for most of the day even before we fucked, and then he stayed until really late that night. We had great conversations and he was really nice. The sex was fine; that I don't feel guilty about. I guess—well—I guess I felt bad because we made a connection. I think I work best when I keep things casual; only sex, no lingering bedroom talk, no eating dinner afterwards, et cetera. Just hooking up and getting off.

Paul's guilt about "connecting" exemplifies once again how important specified fidelity remains for many individuals engaged with multiple sexual partners. He later noted that self-imposed rules become the default when other rules have been violated:

> I guess I just try to do what's best for us. That's my promise to myself. Yeah, I fucked that guy the other night, but it was just to get off. For real. But I was safe about it and I would never do anything to hurt Joe. I know my intentions, and my intentions are

not to fall out of love with him or leave him. I know what I'm doing and why I'm doing it. I trust myself to do what's best for us —even if that means breaking a rule here and there. As long as I'm safe and meet *my* expectations, in the long run, it makes things work so much better for us.

Because rules are established to prevent potential problems from arising and to ensure that partners' needs are being met, breaking the rules becomes a major violation of a formal agreement. Many interviewees discussed eventually forgiving their partners, although some who were nonmonogamous had renegotiated the rules, making them more restrictive for a certain period of time. Molly, a twenty-nine-year-old bisexual woman married to her husband for eight years, revealed her experience with renegotiating her open relationship:

> I had three rules regarding sex with other women: use a condom, not in our house, and tell me about it. Paul broke all three of those rules and ended up giving me a sexually transmitted disease. Thank god it wasn't serious, but damn was I pissed off. So I decided to close the relationship on his end. I still dated other women, but no way in hell was I gonna give him permission to have sex with some other girl.

Ultimately, both monogamists and nonmonogamists reported cheating in various forms. The main difference lies in how nonmonogamists define cheating or refer to such activity in their relationships. Most avoided the term *cheating* in reference to violating agreements. This could be a conscious attempt at resisting value-laden terms, or it could simply be a paradigmatic shift in thinking about relationships and rules. Further, because monogamy implies ownership of a partner's sexuality, resisting concepts that reify sexual ownership could be part of a politicized approach to sexual intimacy. Regardless, it seems that when a rule is broken, renegotiation follows—rather than a more severe response, common in monogamous relationships, such as ending the relationship. This may be because nonmonogamists have already broken the cardinal rule of monogamy; thus, subsequent rule violations may seem less severe and more negotiable than those in monogamous relationships.

Survey data show ways that nonmonogamists responded to cheating in their primary relationships (figures 8a and 8b).

Figure 8a. Primary partner's response to engaging in unallowed behaviors.

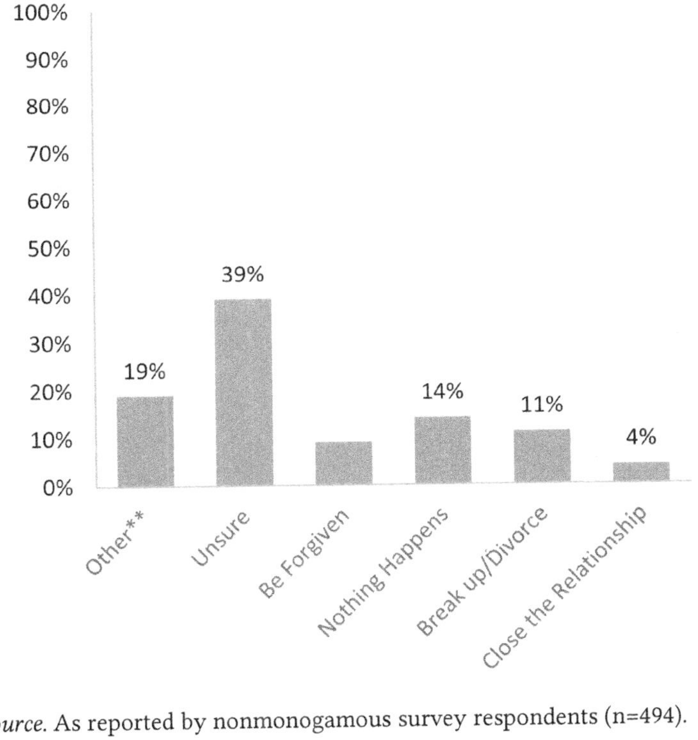

Source. As reported by nonmonogamous survey respondents (n=494).

Most were unsure of the consequences—in part, according to open-ended responses, either because the primary partner had not found out or because a conversation (and perhaps renegotiation) about such violations had yet to be conducted. Further, nonmonogamists were more likely to engage in forgiveness, nothing, or other kinds of responses than to break up or end the relationship. Again, open-ended responses included renegotiation, trial monogamy, and counseling.

Figure 8b. Response to primary partner's engaging in unallowed behaviors.

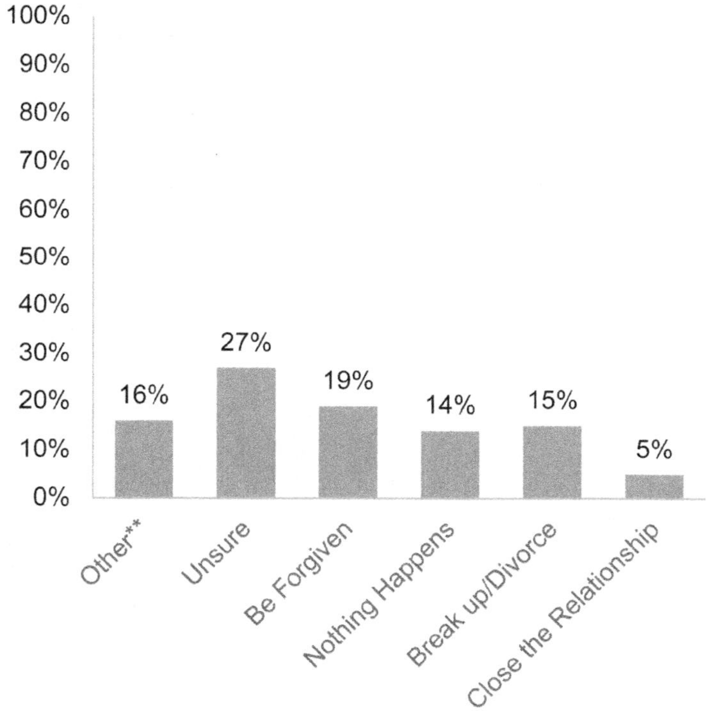

Source. As reported by nonmonogamous survey respondents (n=494).

Several did indicate breaking up or divorce as a consequence. Breaking the rules or engaging in unallowed behaviors is, for most nonmonogamists, a painful experience and still regarded as a form of betrayal and dishonesty; nonmonogamous relationships are not immune to dissolution.

The process of renegotiation exists as a powerful tool in the relationship endeavors of contemporary nonmonogamists and represents a unique form of commitment to the success of the dyad that involves specified fidelity rather than dual exclusivity. Renegotiation is both a consequence of and a reparation to rule violations that exemplifies the choices involved in nonmonogamy because there are no master template constraints on such relationships, no pressure to "act accordingly" when cheating occurs or even when individuals break the rules.

The preceding pages show that although contemporary relationships have in fact diversified in both form and function, the socially prescribed importance of monogamy remains a powerful force. The rules of monogamy have been essentialized through social institutions and social norms, and dual fidelity remains unquestioned by most. The master template of monogamous marriage is thought to provide an arena for achieving love, intimacy, fulfillment, and sexual satisfaction between two individuals, socially legitimating a very specific form of intimate relationships. In other words, the rules have already been established; no need for agreements, contracts, or renegotiations.

The rules of nonmonogamy, however, are not overtly socially scripted; rather, they originate between the individuals themselves who create their own nonmonogamous relationships. Scholars have noted the changing terrain of relationships through behavior and narrative, citing a shift from romance to an emphasis on intimacy that encourages agency in defining, designing, and enacting relationships. Nonmonogamists essentially create their own templates for love and sexual intimacy that further the notion of commitment through specified fidelity. However, as nonmonogamists continue to seek information and advice in structuring their relationships, some agreements and rules have become common fixtures in nonmonogamy.

Surveys of and in-depth interviews with nonmonogamists illustrate that agreements, whether verbal, case by case, or "don't ask, don't tell," are central in structuring alternatives to the master monogamous template. Agreements involve rules that ensure safety and minimize jealousy by regulating certain extradyadic behaviors, certain extradyadic partners, and disclosure about behaviors and potential extradyadic encounters. A fourth category, self-imposed rules, allows a more nuanced version of drawing boundaries that relies upon oneself rather than exchanges with partners. This contributes to a fifth emergent type of fidelity that is most individual in nature, which I discuss in chapter 6. The mere existence of rules serves as a marker of commitment to one another, as well as to the success of the relationship.

A main goal of rule creation and maintenance is to ensure a feeling of specialness between partners. Feeling special involves a certain level of importance or significance that would be achieved through dual fidelity in the traditional master template. In a context in which multiple hearts and bodies entwined, a feeling of uniqueness or specialness appeared to be an important concern for almost all interviewees. If rules are followed, nonmonogamists are able to successfully negotiate the intimacy, love, and sexual connectedness that most, regardless of relationship design, continue to seek. As a result, romantic relationships seem to be becoming more subjective, and individuals operating within the cultural parameters of a new intimacy must balance newfound agency with gendered, heterosexualized scripts that perpetuate traditional monogamy and dual fidelity.

Though the rules of nonmonogamy are agreed upon, individuals do at times violate them. Whereas this is usually characterized as cheating, the phrase *breaking the rules* is more applicable to those who have violated their agreements. This suggests a conscious effort to resist mononormative definitions of rule infringement that rest solely on dual fidelity. Further, when such rules are broken, the consequence is usually a renegotiation of the rules rather than a termination of the relationship, although some instances of rule breaking do in fact result in dissolution. As one participant remarked, "My previous lover and I tried and tried and tried again, but we just couldn't renegotiate anymore." Renegotiation serves as a reminder of commitment to the relationship as well as a deliberate alternative to traditional reactions to cheating, such as breaking up or divorcing. Renegotiation becomes an unexpected yet salient component of the new intimacy deal, and as such, is central in establishing fidelity in contemporary relationships.

Most prior research on consensual nonmonogamy stems from studies conducted in the 1970s on heterosexual swingers, open marriage, and extramarital sex. Within the past few years, a handful of researchers have been expanding the body of literature that addresses the demands of contemporary intimate relationships. This study is at the forefront of a dialogue acknowledging sexual orientation, gender, and diverse relationship forms as necessary considerations in future social science research sampling, analysis, and theorizing. Findings show that whereas gay and bisexual men and bisexual women continue to have higher rates of nonmonogamy, heterosexuals are also incorporating multiple sexual partners into their relationships. The extant research on gay nonmonogamy continues to be informative yet introductory; this study offers a dimension that explores diverse nonmonogamies across sexual orientation and gender.

The rules of nonmonogamy do not always prevent the occurrence of unwanted extradyadic behavior, in the same way that the tenets of dual fidelity and monogamy have been and continue to be violated. However, the rules are perhaps the most significant characteristic of consensual nonmonogamous relationships. They exemplify the way fidelity operates in the form of conscious choices and decisions within the contemporary relationship, offering alternatives to the master monogamous template. The socially recognized, approved, and static contract of marriage predicated upon dual fidelity is clearly not obsolete in the twenty-first century but rather informs nonmonogamy: agreements can be negotiated and renegotiated as needed through specified fidelity. Rules and agreements preserve the fabric of specialness between partners just by existing, and the behaviors they regulate are a clear indication of where the contemporary relationship finds itself: diverse, sexually aware, open to possibilities, flexible in design and execution, and protective of intimacies that rely upon feeling special and significant.

Sexual exclusivity in nonmonogamous relationships is of little concern, but emotional exclusivity is of paramount concern. This pattern emerged in both surveys and interviews, highlighting an explicit resistance to sexual fidelity and an acceptance of emotional fidelity.

This is not the case, however, for those who identify as polyamorous. Although the survey data on nonmonogamists initially included those who identify as polyamorous, I have intentionally excluded their data from this chapter for several reasons. Both survey and interview data highlight a deliberate distinction between nonmonogamy as having mostly multiple sexual (and at times emotional) partners and polyamory as involving both multiple sexual and emotional partners.

ENDNOTES

1. Atwater drew on Erving Goffman for a theoretical explanation of this conflict: "The involvement that an individual sustains within a particular situation is a matter of inward feeling. Assessment of involvement must and does rely on some kind of outward expression. It is here that we can being to analyze the effect of the body idiom, for it is an interesting fact that just as bodily activities seem to be particularly well designed to spread their information through the whole social situation, so also these signs seem well designed to provide information about the individual's involvement. Just as the individual finds that he must convey something through the body idiom and is required to convey the right thing, so also he finds that while present to others he will inevitably convey information about the allocation of his involvement, and that expression of a particular allocation is obligatory" (Goffman 1963, 37).

2. Interviews with individuals and their partners together were avoided in order to collect accurate data and minimize potential conflict. Some interviewees, owing to location and time constraints, requested joint interviews. I agreed with the stipulation that a separate follow-up interview with each individual might be required.

Chapter 5

Many Loves, Multiple Negotiations

Agentic Fidelity and Polyamory

Polyamory coincides with and differs from other types of nonmonogamy in terms of relationship arrangement and function, rules and agreements, ideology, and discourse. It essentially emerged from the sexual revolution and the free-love and rights-based social movements that characterized the 1960s and 1970s (Zell 1990; Noel 2006).[1] Polyamory exists as a relationship structure in which individuals have multiple sexual, emotional, or affective partnerships—and communicate openly about them (Weeks 2011). Within the swinging and open-relationship models, individuals challenge the master monogamous template, engaging with multiple sexual partners and being consensual and overt about such interactions. Polyamory offers an even greater challenge to dual monogamy by recognizing the possibility of multiple *emotional* as well as sexual relations.[2] Based on this capability of multiple loves, polyamorists have actively attempted to distinguish theirs from other forms of nonmonogamy that are based only on multiple sexual interactions.

The language of polyamory becomes a source of concern in that the usual terms and phrases, such as *extramarital sex, dyadic* (and therefore *extradyadic*) *relations,* and even *cheating,* become inherently problematic. Polyamorists characterize their loves and intimacies in the plural, using phrases that clearly subvert the mononormative vocabulary of coupledom. Researching polyamory becomes problematic in terms of recognizing such relationships, employing a research design that incorporates multiple partners, and effectively analyzing data without resorting to mononormative tendencies. This study, therefore, attempts to avoid such oversights in examining fidelity in polyamorous relationships.

This chapter explores the role of fidelity for polyamorists, who explicitly reject traditional relationship arrangements while negotiating alternatives to sexual and emotional exclusivity. If the master monogamous template is subverted, then how (if at all) do polyamorous relationships negotiate love and sex with multiple partners? If emotional fidelity among other nonmonogamists serves to preserve feeling special among multiple partners, then how (if at all) do polyamorists express loyalty and commitment?

Interviewees resisted sexual and emotional exclusivity between partners in both ideology and practice, but the agreements and rules that they had established challenge the notion that "anything goes" in their multiple relationships. In the negotiation, existence, governance, and breaking of rules in polyamorous relationships, it is clear that commitment, loyalty, and specialness resonate with polyamorists. Commitment and specialness among polyamorists are manifest not through exclusivity in love or sex but rather through a more individualized form of loyalty. *Agentic fidelity* requires self-knowledge and the ability and choice to express one's needs, desires, and boundaries to a partner. It also involves individual control in determining and demonstrating commitment and loyalty apart from the traditional tenets of sexual and emotional exclusivity.

The preceding three chapters demonstrate that the structure and "rules" of monogamy are normed and institutionalized, thus providing a template for individuals to engage in sexual or emotional relations with one another. Further, nonmonogamists construct their relationships through rules and agreements, given that there is no socially prescribed master template for multiple partners. This chapter demonstrates the ways the polyamorous approach to fidelity relies not on sexual or emotional exclusivity but rather on an ideology that allows multiple partners while preserving specialness between them. In addition, the rules themselves, rather than what they govern, become the defining characteristic of polyamorous relationships, demonstrating the value, importance, and worth of emotional (albeit multiple) connectedness. The rules give some semblance of power and ultimately indicate commitment simply because they exist. By underscoring their ability for multiple loves, polyamorists reify the value of affective relations more than that of sexual relations. The result is a modified approach to intimate relationships that ensures loyalty not through sexual or emotional facets but rather through the existence of rules and the process of negotiating them.

Polyamorists engage in agentic fidelity by emphasizing a *chosen* loyalty through knowing which rules to establish, choosing when and how to follow them, and effectively articulating among partners a renegotiation of the rules if they are broken. Polyamory invokes a distinct ideology that enables agentic fidelity through emphasis on responsibility, honesty, overt communication, and ethical behavior. However, this ideology is problematic in terms of recognizing the possibility of unethical behavior and rule violation, which has traditionally been described as cheating in monogamous relationships. Finally, by referring to rule violations as breaking the rules rather than as cheating, polyamorists consciously subvert mononormativity not only by structuring their intimate lives but also by constructing alternative narratives for relationship struggles.

Though multiple-partner relationships vary in terms of design, application, and experience, polyamory remains a distinct form of nonmonogamy. Polyamorists have been grouped with other nonmonogamists and glossed over in most sociological literature (see Sheff 2006).[3] The results of this study show that although polyamory is, in fact, one type of nonmonogamy, it exhibits both similarities to and differences from other forms of nonmonogamy in terms of how such relationships are designed, executed, renegotiated (as needed), and ultimately experienced. Further, polyamorists consciously distance themselves from other forms of nonmonogamy, both in ideology and practice. Survey and interview data indicate a pattern of creating formal agreements, establishing rules, and navigating them (in terms of both following and breaking them, much as among nonmonogamists). However, the results indicate that for polyamorists, communication, disclosure, and honesty are interwoven into the overall ethos of multiple-partner relations. Polyamorists explicitly resist sexual and emotional exclusivity while maintaining commitment through agentic fidelity in their relationships. This is achieved through exercising choice in constructing the rules, understanding the overall process of creating agreements, and focusing on the existence of rules, rather than on what they govern, as indicators of commitment.

THE POLYAMOROUS PROCESS: FORMULATING AGREEMENTS ABOUT MULTIPLE PARTNERS

Survey results from 343 polyamorous individuals indicate that, much like other nonmonogamists, an overwhelming majority of polyamorists have some kind of agreement about which extradyadic activities are or are not allowed with others, whether it is verbal (65%), case by case (15%), written (8%), or "don't ask, don't tell" (1%). Several (19%) described other types of agreements in their open-ended comments:

> We have a written poly contract that specifies openness in general, but specific case/time management is negotiated verbally.
>
> —Heterosexual male

> My lover lives with me and my husband and my husband's lover comes over every other weekend and on the in-between weekends he goes there. When we were more actively seeking other partners (before these long-term relationships), we had both verbal agreements and written safe-sex agreements.
>
> —Heterosexual female

> The safer sex agreements are case by case.
>
> —Bisexual female

> Some general rules are set out verbally, but each potential partner is to be discussed individually.
>
> —Heterosexual male

Many open-ended responses exemplify a combination of verbal, written, and case-by-case agreements. However, some survey responses indicated agreements that were tailored more to individuals and their specific relationships:

> No formal agreement, but lots of discussion and in-depth check-ins! We trust each other to make the right choices. We do like to talk about those choices.
>
> —Heterosexual male

> We have forged our own "Sexual Credo."
>
> —Heterosexual female

> We have an understanding. There are no fixed parameters other than to be kind to each other and kind to others.
>
> —Bisexual male

> We are in constant conversation about what each other is doing
> and what we would like to do.
>
> —Bisexual female

Although their types of agreements are similar to those of
nonmonogamists, polyamorists have higher rates of written contracts,
case-by-case agreements, and other kinds of agreements. Other forms
of nonmonogamy favor "don't ask, don't tell" policies, verbal agreements, and no set accords about multiple partners. Such disparity is the
first of several in comparing polyamory with other nonmonogamies;
full disclosure, total honesty, and routine check-ins are common among
polyamorists and are further represented in the interview data. Total
honesty and full disclosure are concepts predicated upon the notion of
overt and consensual multiple partners, answering any and all questions
about behaviors, thoughts, opinions, and preferences. Many polyamorists consider these central to their partnerships, although the frequency
and degree of engagement varies.

Several survey responses invoked a more autonomous approach to
agreements about multiple partners, problematizing the existence of an
agreement:

> Because we respect each other's autonomy and judgment, we have
> no formal "agreement"; however, we *agree* on critical issues.
> Even should we disagree, however, we are careful to arrange
> things that the choices of one person will not harm the other. For
> instance, we practice "safe sex" with each other, even though we
> are primary to each other, so that if one person makes an error in
> judgment, or has an accident, it has no consequence for the other
> person ... Neither of us would ever presume to tell the other who
> they could or could not relate to.
>
> —Bisexual female

> We don't need an agreement ... we *know* we are not exclusive to
> each other.
> —Heterosexual male

> We don't put limits on what we do with other people. The only
> agreement is that we are respectful and kind to each other when
> we are with each other, and keep in contact the rest of the time.
> —Heterosexual female

Although to some an agreement represented control, limitation, and
restriction reminiscent of the master monogamous template, these individuals were in the minority. Most polyamorists had an agreement of
some sort, even if it was to have no rules or restrictions about others. In
addition, over one-third (39%) indicated at some point their resistance to
using terms like *allow*, *restrict*, and *rules* through open-ended answers to
particular questions. Some even wrote comments in the margins of the
survey. The following are typical survey remarks:

> It is not my place to allow or put restrictions on my partners.
> —Bisexual male

> I do not give my partners lists of allowed and prescribed behav-
> iors. Instead, I tell my partners that I expect them to be honest with
> me at all times in all things, including in their dealings with others;
> that I expect them to be compassionate and sensitive to my needs
> and feelings; and I expect them to be responsible with respect to
> my sexual health, their sexual health, and the sexual health of all
> their partners. Provided that I feel my needs from the relationship
> are met and that they are behaving honestly and responsibly, they
> are able to determine for themselves what actions they engage in.
> —Bisexual female

This bisexual female's comments indicate that there are still rules,
but they are framed in terms of expectations and standards that are
both emotional and behavioral. Respondents' resistance to allowances
or restrictions demonstrates that for many polyamorists, confronting

normative sexual ownership and emotional property is an ethical concern in approaching their intimate relationships. However, most still had some sort of agreement.

A few (4%) respondents indicated that they had no formal agreement about interactions or behaviors. This was often related to the stage of a certain relationship, concerns about privacy or secrecy, and for some, their status as secondary partner:

> We are early in the relationship (several weeks) and haven't worked it out yet, although the topic is "on the table."
> —Bisexual male

> He doesn't know about my other partners, so no agreement.
> —Heterosexual female

> I'm only a secondary—I don't have a say in anything. He's my primary, but I'm only his secondary. I either take what is offered or I leave. No negotiations. No agreements. And certainly *no* veto power. I don't want him to have other partners other than me and his primary, but what I want doesn't matter, since I'm only a secondary.
> —Heterosexual female

Many nonmonogamous relationships utilize a primary/secondary structure, wherein primary partners are dyadic and secondary partners operate more in terms of satellite relations. For a number of polyamorists, however, the mere use of the terms *primary* and *secondary* conflicts with the polyamorist ideology in that multiple primaries are common and partners should not be hierarchical.

Because most survey respondents (96%) had some sort of agreement with their partners concerning behaviors with others, results clearly show that polyamorous relationships are far from "anything goes." Both survey and interview data detail a range of behaviors and interactions that such agreements mediate. As discussed in chapters 3 and 4, survey respondents were asked to indicate which types of behaviors were "allowed" with others. Both monogamists and nonmonogamists indicated dancing as the most acceptable interaction and falling in love with someone else as the least acceptable. This may reflect individuals' preserving emotional exclusivity as the key component to maintaining fidelity—whether dual, veiled, or specified—between partners.

Polyamorists, however, indicated quite different allowed behaviors. Kissing was the most acceptable interaction with others (over 90%), and a majority (over 80%) both allowed and were allowed by partners to hold hands, dance, use hands for stimulation, receive oral stimulation, give oral stimulation, and engage in threesomes or group sexual experiences (figure 9). Most allowed partners (84%) and were allowed (90%) to fall in love with others. Given that polyamory is predicated upon the ability and opportunity to love in multiples, restricting or being restricted from falling in love with other partners essentially contradicts polyamorist ideology. Nevertheless, some indicated that either they were not allowed or did not allow their partners to fall in love with others. Open-ended responses indicate that this could relate to polyfidelitous relationships or "closed" triads or quads that restrict emotional (and sometimes sexual) involvement with new or other partners. Vaginal penetration, spending the night, and anal penetration were the most restricted interactions. Open-ended responses suggest that this may relate to issues regarding safe sex, pregnancy, and for some, resistance to sharing extended time with other partners.

Some survey respondents indicated other allowed (35%) and allowable (30%) activities in open-ended format. This is another difference between polyamorists and both monogamists and nonmonogamists: polyamorists reported a wide range of other activities that involved sexual, emotional, financial, and spiritual relations.

Figure 9. Percentage of polyamorous survey respondents indicating allowable/allowed activities with others.

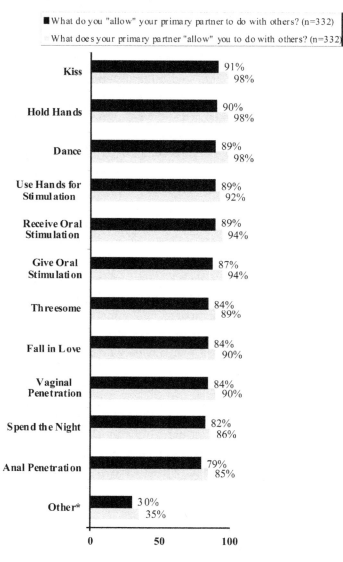

Many of these activities also involved elements of kink and BDSM (bondage, dominance/discipline, sadism, masochism): adult consensual erotic or disciplinary spanking, bondage and restraint, related arts such as kink play and vagina fisting; touching, flogging, being flogged, tantric practice, sex parties, spanking; S&M (sadism and masochism) D&S (dominance and submission) activities, piercing fetishes and a shoe fetish.[4] Other allowed activities included the option to use sex toys, play board games, flirt, hug, exchange nonromantic kisses, snuggle, give and receive (nonsexual) massage, go out to dinner or the movies, cook together, and as one respondent indicated, engage in "any epidemiologically safe activity."

Overall, survey data show that neither sexual nor emotional interactions between multiple partners are heavily restricted. Yet this is not an indication that anything goes regarding acceptable behaviors with other partners; most polyamorists do have agreements or rules of some sort. The glaring difference between polyamorists and other nonmonogamists is that polyamory (by definition) does not restrict multiple sexual, romantic, or affective partners, although their agreements and rules do ensure agentic fidelity and negotiate needs and boundaries in multiple partnerships.

RULES AND REGULATIONS IN POLYAMOROUS RELATIONSHIPS

Polyamorous interviewees, like other nonmonogamists, described rules about behaviors with other partners. As discussed in chapter 4, nonmonogamists enact rules that restrict certain sexual and nonsexual activities based on safe-sex concerns, efforts to maintain primary pair bonds, and the desire to "feel special." Such rules exemplify a distinction between embracing multiple sexual partners and maintaining emotional fidelity. Polyamorists also establish similar rules concerning safe sex, at times with even more vigilance than other nonmonogamists.

For example, William, a thirty-three-year-old bisexual involved in a polyamorist commune with four other partners, stated:

> We have an explicit rule that there has to be STD testing before any sexual contact with a new partner. That means no impulsive going to clubs to hook up and have sex. If something like that were to happen, there would be definite consequences in terms of how long we all would have to go without sexual contact before test results can be obtained. We have a group of people who have to be protected here; we rely on each other to protect each other.

As in the interviews, an overwhelming majority (91%) of open-ended polyamorous survey responses reflected safer sex concerns in comments such as "Safe sex is a must" and "No condom, no penetration."

In addition to safer sex rules, polyamorists also described rules about overnight dates or spending the night with others, as nonmonogamous interviewees did. Incidentally, they also indicated "spending the night" as one of the least allowable/allowed activities with others. Whereas one interviewee spoke of practical concerns, such as needing to use the family car the next morning, most who had rules about overnights described them in terms of drawing emotional boundaries, as Peter, Timothy, and Katie did:

> We had a rule about sleeping over at someone else's place. I was not to spend the night and she wasn't able to spend the night at another lover's place. It was actually more her rule than mine, but I appreciated having the extra time with her.
>
> —Peter, 23, heterosexual

> Our only other rule besides safe sex is that we agreed on no overnight dates with other people.
>
> —Timothy, 22, gay

> The main rule was whatever we did we would end up in our bed at the end of the evening. And what that ended up meaning was that at the end of the day, we would be in bed together and start

telling each other what we did and we would get so turned on we
would end up making love.

—Katie, 32, bisexual

Though sexual safety and overnights remained the most central issues
in rules about behavior, interviewees were least likely to restrict various
types of sexual interaction with others. A few commented that their first
multiple-partner experiences had included rules and agreements about
vaginal penetration or even anal sex, but in subsequent relationships
such rules had dissipated.

Unlike their nonmonogamous counterparts, polyamorists rarely spoke
of regulating certain sexual activities or of restricting particular behaviors. Instead, interviewees and survey respondents described agreements
about what partners *should* do rather than what they should not do.
These rules fell into two main categories central to a polyamorous
ideology: communication and disclosure.

Rules about Communication: Enforcing Sincerity and Honesty

Interviewees repeatedly discussed polyamory as essentially predicated
upon continual communication with all partners involved. As one joked,
"We spend more time *communicating* about having sex and falling in
love than actually having sex and falling in love!" Communication can
include a vast array of styles and degrees, and it concerns a multitude
of issues, but many interviewees had agreements about communication
in terms of logistical concerns and translating desires and boundaries.
Interviewees conferred basics like scheduling dates and play times and
coordinating family gatherings:

> My friend teases me because I have this planner I use for my dates
> with all my partners [pulls out planner with color-coded names,
> locations, and lists of "what to pack" scribbled on a monthly
> calendar]. It is totally anal retentive, but it really helps me keep
> track! I swear people don't realize how hard polyamory is in terms

of making time for everyone. Maybe *I'm* just exceptionally busy [laughs]. But we actually have a rule about communication about scheduling issues since there are essentially five of us to deal with.
—Heather, 29, bisexual

We both struggle with scheduling, so one of our agreements is to be good about communicating our schedules. I'm more flexible than Alex because I don't have kids, so in order for us to make time for each other, we constantly are checking in about plans, events, and commitments.
—Margie, 38, heterosexual

Polyamorists related that communicating logistics with partners is imperative both in negotiating multiple relationships and in making sure individuals are getting the time they need and want with each other.

Communication also involves prioritizing discussions about any agreements or rules between partners. Both Peter and Molly suggested that communication about contentment or dissatisfaction with the rules is an integral part of polyamory. Peter, a twenty-three-year-old heterosexual former swinger turned polyamorist, described communication as "*the* poly core" and suggested that a strong sense of self helps facilitate communication:

It's really important if you're going to do any of this poly stuff that you have a really strong sense of yourself, who you are, what you want, and where your boundaries are. That's hard enough to do in any relationship, but if you're doing polyamory, it's really, really important. The key is communicating that strong sense of self, what you want, who you are, and what your boundaries are to your partner.

Molly, a twenty-nine-year-old heterosexual woman involved with two male partners, commented that one must be aware of one's desires and boundaries before she or he can effectively communicate them to another partner:

> Polyamory challenges me to grow. Sometimes it pushes me beyond my comfort zone, and it's not always comfortable, but I like it; I like that I'm challenged to grow. I like that it makes me question myself and look at, you know, look at what I'm feeling and what I'm thinking and where it comes from. That way I can communicate my needs to my partners and be able to articulate exactly what I need and want. Like if I feel jealousy or if I feel insecurity, I can tell them why I feel like I do, what is setting me off, and we can work together to get beyond it.

Like Molly, other interviewees and survey respondents identified self-awareness as a necessary central component to effective communication. Though good communication seems to be the default suggestion for making any relationship (monogamous or nonmonogamous) succeed, polyamorous interviewees emphasized communication as the core component of a multiple-partner paradigm. A few long-term polyamorists even described the "poly mantra" as "Communicate, communicate, and then communicate more!" Polyamorists seemed to emphasize a *commitment* to communication more than they stressed communication itself. Many cited resources—for instance, poly websites, books such as *The Ethical Slut*, and local poly networks—that provide support for facilitating open communication, establishing rules, recognizing desires, and respecting boundaries. "With open, honest communication," said Wendell, "anything, or *anyone*, is possible!"

Rules about Disclosure: Staying Overt and Open

Polyamorists usually have disclosure rules that encourage (or sometimes restrict) revealing interest in a potential partner, an upcoming date, or details about a recent encounter. As one survey respondent commented,

> We don't have rules that say, oh you can't have intercourse with so-and-so or you can only have oral with me. It's like we focus more on the positive rather than the negative—agreements that focus on what we *should* be doing as opposed to what we're *not supposed* to be doing. Our only real rule is about disclosing who

we want to be with, what we've done, and what we'd like to do
with somebody!

—Heterosexual male

Most interviewees and open-ended survey respondents had rules about
discussing behavioral details and disclosure in varying degrees and
contexts:

> Anthony prefers to know beforehand if it's likely to happen, but
> we also acknowledge that there might be occasions where, like if
> we go out of town or we meet someone and in a flurry have sex
> with them, then we tell the person after the fact. But the prefer-
> ence is to know ahead of time.
>
> —Molly, 29, heterosexual

> I can always be with other females with or without his knowledge
> ... He is only supposed to be with females if I know about them.
>
> —Bisexual female

> Another rule was that we would not let the children know about
> it. And that rule actually turned out to be a mistake, because it
> turns out that children know more than we think and they figure
> things out ... I went to pick up my wife and son at the airport
> after a recent visit to her other lover. When we were waiting for
> the luggage, my son shouted, "I saw mommy in the shower with
> Bruce!" We were standing underneath this cone-shaped fixture
> hanging from the airport ceiling, and it completely magnified
> what my son had said. Essentially, the whole luggage area heard
> about mommy's other lover.
>
> —Oden, 35, heterosexual

> We have a non-specific but verbal agreement allowing each other
> to see whoever else we wish to, as long we keep each other
> informed (but not necessarily of all the gory details).
>
> —Heterosexual female

Polyamorists sometimes mentioned full disclosure or total honesty in
describing their arrangements about communication. This can refer to

communicating about activities or interactions with certain partners, negotiating rules, or relaying satisfaction and dissatisfaction with any agreements or individuals. Full disclosure and total honesty are key concepts in maintaining a polyamorous framework. They allow individuals a certain amount of agency in expressing their needs, articulating their desires, and describing their behaviors. They also provide a context for receiving similar information from one's partners.

Addressing both disclosure and total honesty, participants also described veto power as a common element. Veto power is the ability to disapprove of (and therefore hinder relations with) another's potential partner:

> Our policy is that we must get permission for each new partner we may choose to take, prior to sexual activity with that person. We can veto secondary partners at any time. Our existing secondary partners also must be informed of any new partners prior to sexual activity, and their concerns heard and discussed, but they don't get automatic veto privileges.
>
> —Bisexual female

> My primary partner has "veto power," but it is understood that the veto is only to be used in extreme circumstances. Otherwise, he'll be vetoing every freakin' partner I wanna have sex with!
>
> —Katie, 32, heterosexual

> I can veto his outside partners if I want.
>
> —Heterosexual female

> With one of my partners, we don't really have an agreement, other than that any protected sexual activity is okay. With my other partner, we have an agreement to disclose any other sexual activities or dates that we have. In one case he asked me not to have sex with a couple (as a threesome) again because he was not comfortable with the situation and felt that the STD risk was high. But I've not used my veto power with him.
>
> —Bisexual female

Simply having veto power was enough for certain interviewees, who felt as though the ability to have input in their partners' engagements acknowledged commitment between individuals. Interviewees used the rules of communication and disclosure as a forum for establishing commitment, as well as for encouraging total honesty with oneself and between partners. Whereas other nonmonogamists seemed to enact rules for the sake of preventing misbehavior and encouraging revelation, polyamorists treated honesty as more of an ethical concern inherent in a polyamorous lifestyle.

Overall, the agreements and rules that polyamorists described in survey and interview responses reflect a responsibility to both communicate and disclose. Again, it seems that their rules are less regulatory and more participatory, encouraging an overall commitment to oneself, current partners, and potential partners rather than restricting certain sexual and nonsexual interactions. Further, those who were vehement regarding no rules about "anything other than safe sex" underscore the possibility, rather than the restriction, of multiple sexual and emotional interconnections.

Though the rule categories are fairly similar to those of other nonmonogamists, polyamorist rules about communication and disclosure serve an additional function, preserving agentic fidelity between partners. Self-awareness is key in being able to articulate one's needs and boundaries; it also is necessary in knowing how to best receive similar information from other partners. Through agreements and rules, polyamorists both adopt and perpetuate an ideology dichotomized against mononormativity, which empowers individuals to demonstrate loyalty to a polyamorous ideology and commitment to one's partners through agentic fidelity. Polyamorists spend a considerable amount of time and energy communicating about relationships, partners, agreements, and rules. However, some follow the rules, and others break them. Even in breaking the rules, polyamorists contribute another dimension to contemporary fidelities that involves reframing cheating in terms of both behavior and consequence.

"I Didn't Cheat; I Just Broke the Rules": Resistance to Mononormative Notions of Infidelity through Polyamorous Accounting Schemas

For most interviewees, establishing agreements and creating rules seemed to be a relatively easy part of polyamory; actually following them proved to be a different story. Both survey and interview data show that a fair number had breached their agreements, but many participants stressed that they followed their established rules:

> I can honestly say I follow our rules. We only had a couple to begin with, like safe sex, wanting to meet each other's potential partners, honesty, et cetera. If I didn't follow the rules, it would just be like a purely pleasure-seeking thing. It wouldn't be like we had a relationship that requires a certain amount of work, and here's what we're going to do to make it happen. It would be like I just feel like doing this and I don't have to answer to you for anything. Anything in life worth having is worth working for, and relationships are no exception to that. That's why I follow the rules. Rules create trust, which makes it more easy for you to be more open and to be able to give more, knowing that you've created some kind of security together. The relationship itself becomes a safe container for you to experience and feel things without feeling the threat of that going away. Rules are the glue that holds the safe container together.
>
> —Peter, 41, heterosexual

> I value love, respect, and integrity in a relationship. Actually, honesty is the highest value for me. Breaking the rules is a really dishonest, disrespectful, and deceitful thing to do to someone.
>
> —Molly, 45, heterosexual

I don't break rules. I follow them. That's why I created them in the first place.

—Bisexual male

> I have some poly friends who always seem to be breaking their rules. I joke that we have, like, *no* limits on sex, fucking, love, all that stuff, yet they *still* manage to break some rule about something. It's like, c'mon you guys. Don't mess up the great thing we have here because you're too fucking lazy to use a rubber.
>
> —Timothy, 22, gay

I asked each interviewee if they had ever broken the rules. Some responded that they had not broken the rules of their current relationships or those of previous relationships. But most either acknowledged or alluded to rule infractions. Interviewees were, at times, a bit hesitant to admit such behaviors because of embarrassment or complicated situations and because they felt that revealing such information would tarnish the open and allowing reputation of polyamory.

Danika spoke of her agreements, rules, and following (and eventually breaking) them, revealing a more complicated picture of polyamory. An articulate forty-year-old bisexual woman, Danika was involved with three lovers: Valentino, a married man who had recently been "taken down a few notches," Aaron, her business partner and regular lover, and Tara, a new partner she was exploring through a BDSM relationship. Danika described herself as currently "dating poly style," meaning that she could connect with people at any level of intimacy that felt right for her without this alienating the other people. I asked why Valentino had recently been "taken down a few notches":

> Valentino, his wife and I were actually in a triad that we recently ended, but I still do see Valentino, just not his wife. We lived together, and there were some agreements between us concerning our relationship—and we had a huge emotionally draining fight and we put the agreements in place so it wouldn't be that way.

When I asked her to describe the agreements with Valentino, she replied, "You know what, I think I'd rather not say." She did, however describe her agreements with both Aaron and Tara:

> Aaron and I have the agreement that if you end up having unprotected sex with somebody, let me know before you touch me again so we can plot our course because we are fluid-bonded. And also, just sort of let each other know, loosely, when new people come on the horizon. He and I have a similar mindset where we're able to hold each other really loosely. Valentino is the one who wants to know everything all the time, which kind of drives me crazy. With Tara, I'm trying to ferret out our rules since our relationship is new. If I'm going to play with someone else, BDSM or sexually, she would like to know if advance if possible. Um, I assume it's common courtesy that we tell each other about fluid bondings; like if there has been a change, I let them know. And in certain times and in certain spaces, Tara gets totally authority over me. Another rule is that I can't dominate Tara.

Throughout the interview, Danika spoke of her struggles with Valentino and his wife, Penelope, vis-à-vis ensuring that her own needs were met while managing the tumultuous situation with the wife. She felt as though Valentino continually put his wife before her, even encouraging Danika to buy a house that Danika and Valentino would share and later rescinding, stating, "Penelope just doesn't like it." In responding to a question about breaking rules, Danika revealed:

> So basically, before I got Valentino's permission, I began having unprotected sex with Aaron, and continued for at least a couple months before I even said anything. This of course was not my proudest moment, but I'm just being completely honest with you. What good is research if people don't tell the truth, right?

After thanking Danika for her honesty, I proceeded to ask what implications her interaction with Aaron had for the agreements she established with Valentino:

> [Hesitates] Yeah, this was really our most important agreement, because he and Penelope were fluid-bonded. Like I said, most of the time I'm a person of integrity. I feel really bad about it. I've never told Valentino about it, I'm not gonna tell him, and that's kind of why I didn't talk about our agreements before with you. I'm like, this will never happen with anybody ever again; I will never do this again. I've given myself a real strong admonition; I wouldn't want anybody to treat me that way and I don't want to treat anybody that way. Two or three months of not telling someone something like that is not cool in my book.

Danika used the phrase *fluid-bonded*, which refers to partners who engage in unprotected sex and usually signifies a certain level of commitment and intimacy. Other interviewees described partners who became fluid-bonded only after undergoing rigorous sexually transmitted disease and infection testing and adhering to a total-honesty policy. Danika's decision to have unprotected sex with Aaron carried several implications for all parties involved, both physically and emotionally. I asked Danika why she had made the decision to engage in and continue to have unprotected sex:

> Well, it was kind of in the heat of the moment, middle of the night, you know, suddenly we realized, oh crap. And then I was gonna have the conversation with Valentino right away and tell him, but he was such a shit to me with the house situation, and it wasn't like I wanted to intentionally hurt him, it was just bad timing. And I was enjoying the connection and fluid-bonding with Aaron so much that I guess I didn't want to give it up. That's when I sort of took things down a few notches with Valentino, and started using barriers with them both again.

Danika said that she continued to follow the rules she had established with both Aaron and Tara, her new interest. She later confirmed, again, that she was a person of integrity and that she had "made a mistake" in breaking the rules. Nevertheless, her story acknowledges that polyamorous individuals can and do sometimes break the rules of their relationships.

Although cheating and other forms of rule violations seem to be of paramount concern in monogamous relationships, secretive nonconsensual activities occur even in nonmonogamous and polyamorous relationships. In chapter 4, I discuss nonmonogamists who characterize such behavior in terms of breaking the rules rather than in terms of infidelity or cheating. Informed by this pattern, I asked specifically polyamorous interviewees if they had ever cheated on their partners:

> What a good question, because by definition it's almost a contradiction in terms. I can't say that I have cheated. Generally, I think that there are some people who "do poly" a whole lot better than others. And there are lots of different shades of poly. I've seen people that identify as poly and what they were doing certainly didn't look like poly to me! I guess to me if you have rules and then break those rules, you've cheated. But I don't like that term because, again, it's a contradiction since cheating implies [stops midsentence, with a blank stare]—well, it's like "pseudo-cheating." You are 'cause you're breaking rules but you aren't because the rules are different than normal rules about monogamy.
>
> —Molly, 29, heterosexual

> I think it's really lame that you make up your own rules and you can't even keep them. I've seen it happen, and it's happened to me. Even with monogamy, there's a bunch of assumed rules. And people break those—so polys really aren't that different. Well, I guess the good thing about polyamory is it makes you examine what's important to you and what's not, like where my boundaries are.
>
> —Peter, 23, heterosexual

> I haven't really broken the rules, but I sort of bent them. We had a rule about sleepovers, but I was—well, I kind of fell asleep after I had sex with someone. I ended up driving home at, like, five a.m.

hoping Hannah wouldn't be pissed. It was clearly not intentional, and I didn't spend the whole night away.

—Martin, 29, heterosexual

According to survey data, polyamorous respondents do report cheating on their current primary partner(s). Results show that 18% had cheated on their current partners, whereas 12% reported that their primary partners had cheated on them (table 9).

Table 9. Survey respondents' reported rates of cheating in nonmonogamous and polyamorous relationships.

Have You Cheated on Your Current Partner?

	Nonmonogamous N=512	Polyamorous N=343
Yes	38%	18%
No	61	80
Refused to Answer	*	2

Has Your Current Partner Cheated on You?

	Nonmonogamous N=512	Polyamorous N=343
Yes	27%	12%
No	70	86
Refused to Answer	2	2

*Less than 1%

It is important to again note that several survey respondents expressed discontent with the terminology used in the survey and that this may have affected the validity of the survey results. Several wrote elaborate comments explicating that cheating is for monogamists and others who are not "honest and open" about their multiple partners.[5] However, polyamorists' cheating rates are fairly similar to those of nonmonogamists and even monogamists.

"Let's Reconsider": Rule Renegotiations and Reevaluations

Both nonmonogamous and polyamorous interviewees discussed the consequences of rule infractions as involving renegotiation rather than termination of the relationship(s). Survey data show that an overwhelming majority (87%) of polyamorists indicated renegotiation as the primary response to either engaging in or finding out about a partner's engagement in activities "not allowed" with others. Peter offered his conclusions as to why polyamorists break the rules and, instead of terminating a relationship, engage in renegotiation:

> Rules in poly relationships don't have as strong of a hold over the individual like they do in, say, traditional marriage. With traditional marriage, there's this idea that it's a sacrament and you're involved in something bigger than yourself. With poly, it's very much about your wants and your partner's wants. We make rules, see how it works, get rid of the old rules, and make some new ones —and they may change again. Since the rules can and do change, I think the rules seem less concrete, which seems to have less hold over someone, so rules wind up getting broken, and people cheat.

At first, Peter suggested that one reason polyamorists break the rules may have to do with the rules themselves not seeming concrete because they have not been institutionalized as the rules of monogamy have. He subsequently questioned his use of the term *cheating*:

Cheating seems so serious—like in a monogamous marriage, cheating is a big deal because they both have this mutual rule of sexual fidelity. But with poly, the rules are more unique to the person. So if someone breaks a rule, it may not seem like cheating to them because the rule itself didn't seem important to them. Of course, for the other person who made the rule, it's a clear violation and can be devastating. It's more about following someone's wishes and respecting their boundaries than actually engaging in the behavior.

Peter's responses, like those of many others, indicate that part of polyamory is recognizing that rules both come into existence and occasionally need to be renegotiated or reevaluated. This process may seem less concrete than relying on socially normed relationship rules. At the same time, rule violations also seem less detrimental because such rules can be and are often renegotiated. Yet polyamorists expressed frustration and discontent with the rules; no matter how or what the rules restrict, potential for conflict was always present.

Christina, a thirty-three-year-old bisexual woman, had been dating a single man as a primary partner for over five years and had also been involved with a married couple for over four years. Christina described herself as the poster child of polyamory, citing years of experience with multiple loves, heartbreaks, and sexual exploits; she had a great deal of advice to give to "poly newbies." We met at a coffee shop for the interview and stayed until the place closed, finishing the last few questions on a nearby bench several hours later. Toward the end of the interview, Christina described a current struggle with Jenni and Marshall, the married couple she was dating:

I'm frustrated because right now nobody gets an overnight date. They are both in marriage counseling, not because things are going bad, but because Jenni has some communication stuff to work through. She is not feeling very secure right now so she just doesn't want him gone overnight with me. I can understand that, so it doesn't bother me too much, although come to think of it, it has been going on for a while. Maybe it's time to reevaluate the sleepover situation.

Renegotiations and reevaluations serve the purpose of recognizing that individuals' needs and desires within relationships are not static. Polyamorists exhibited an understanding of this fluctuation that monogamists and even some other nonmonogamists did not. Though most appreciated the opportunities to try and try again to make their boundaries and limitations known and to see them addressed (through agreements, rules, or simply the freedom to state them), one interviewee in particular expressed his distaste for such efforts:

> The thing I dislike most about poly is having to always renegotiate and check in. It's like we're always talking about this and that and what we want to do and what she wants to do and how I'm going to meet those needs and how she can better meet mine. Sometimes I feel like we spend more time discussing our relationship than enjoying our relationship. *Everything* has to be processed before, during, and after.
>
> —Martin, 29, heterosexual

Overall, renegotiation seems to be the rubric for handling rule infractions, conflict, and disagreements in both nonmonogamous and, to a greater extent, polyamorous relationships. Reevaluation seems to be the forum for examining both individual and collective relationship goals; it allows both disagreement and resolution as needed. Further, simply communicating about one's relationship with a partner or partners can be a way of spending time together and unifying efforts to maximize the relationship's potential. In other words, the *process* of establishing and renegotiating rules is a key component to agentic fidelity—that is, the commitment to and loyalty in making arrangements together about the relationship.

PRESERVING SPECIALNESS THROUGH AGENTIC FIDELITY

Having multiple sexual or emotional partners can be, at times, rather taxing. Feeling special is ultimately an articulation of pair bonding or of sharing something unique between individuals; many nonmonogamists preserve this specialness through specified fidelity—namely, emotional exclusivity. Specialness remains salient for polyamorists, and is confirmed in several studies on polyamory (Keener 2004; Cook 2005). Survey and interview data in this study highlight that many have the need to feel special or to share unique behaviors, interactions, or even locations with certain partners. Christina said that lacking such specialness could be the drive behind jealousy:

> I had a friend once who told me that people feel jealous because they are lacking something—like time or some other kind of specialness with someone. It's not that I'm jealous of her [Jenni], but she and Marshall have gone on a few overnight trips and I don't get to do that. I feel bad that I feel jealous, but then I don't know if it is jealousy or envy. Jealousy to me means that you don't want the other person doing it—*you* want to be doing it instead. Or is that envy? Well, either way I feel like someone else is getting all the good stuff and I'm stuck by myself at home. I feel left out and someone else is getting the attention that I want and need.

Whereas Jenni's rule about no overnight dates served to minimize her jealousy and ensure her feeling secure, Christina expressed that *she* felt jealous as a result. Christina and I spent considerable time discussing her distinctions between jealousy and envy and that jealousy, to her, was a necessary yet manageable evil of multiple-partner relationships. Although Christina initially resisted the notion of specialness, her subsequent reflection on what just she and Marshall did together indicates that specialness remained salient for her: "Marshall and I have this spot on the beach where we set up a blanket with wine, and it's really romantic and something special we share." Spending time, engaging in particular behaviors, and sharing moments with certain partners become primary contexts for specialness. Both open-ended survey and interviewee responses indicate that some agreements and rules exist to preserve this form of exclusivity:

> Our only rule besides safe sex is that we don't engage in behaviors that would interfere with the time we spend together.
>
> —Heterosexual male

> Here are our rules: (1) Don't bring home diseases—safe sex. (2) If the person we want to do something with says "no," then "no" means "no." (3) Treat everyone the way you want to be treated. (4) Outside relationships should not have a significant negative effect on the primary relationship and our family.
>
> —Heterosexual female

> I like getting attention from a lot of different men. I like the freedom to be with other people sexually, and I like that I can talk to Jay about other men that I've been involved with and get support and feedback from him. He kind of gets included in this way where he's not directly involved but is able to participate through sharing advice and being my friend. We enjoy that aspect of connecting with each other.
>
> —Molly, 29, heterosexual

> One rule is not to put others' needs ahead of our own, and to make time for just each other, even if it is brief, because we need to put energy into maintaining our bond.
>
> —Bisexual female

In addition to rules specifically about retaining specialness, separate rules about no sleepover dates or spending the night often referred, once again, to the notion of specialness—such activities were usually reserved for primary or particular partners, such as secondaries. Although some study participants embraced specialness as a form of commitment between partners, a few resisted the notion of specialness, especially given that it operates as a construct inherent in monogamous relationship design. Wendell, a fifty-seven-year-old bisexual man who had recently left a marriage and was beginning a new relationship with a woman, discussed the rule his last wife had about kissing other partners:

> She didn't want anyone kissing me on the mouth because she wanted to be just as safe from cold germs as from any other disease. And she really strongly believed in having things that were just special between us, which I don't believe in, and so she managed to structure things so that kissing would be the one thing that was, uh, special. Exclusive between us.

Wendell's account was unique in that most interviewees described sharing something special with their partners, even if it was minor in content or significance. I asked Wendell what he meant when he said he did not believing in having things special with his partners:

> I just like being loving and being loving with whoever I feel compatible with. Lovingness that doesn't have restrictions like kissing or special things with some and not others. Monogamous marriage has restrictions like this. You have to be in love with your one soul mate and think and feel for only them. They are special, and you are special, and no one else matters.

Whereas Wendell felt limited behaviorally and ideologically by the notion of specialness in terms of his behavior, it seems that most polyamorous respondents approached feeling special as an integral part of having multiple partners. Whether the notion of specialness is in fact an archetype of mononormativity, the rules of polyamory indicate that specialness is one way that individuals engage in commitment with other partners. Monogamists use dual fidelity in order to achieve and reflect commitment. Nonmonogamists use behavioral rules and emotional monogamy to ensure fidelity. Polyamorists use emotional rules to essentially choose how to construct their fidelities with multiple partners, given that sexual and emotional exclusivity are no longer salient. This results in agentic fidelity; individuals decide what makes them feel special and unique between partners.

Polyamorists approach agentic fidelity in two contexts: the first is a more traditional use of fidelity in terms of sexual and emotional commitment between partners involved in polyamorous relationships together, termed *polyfidelity*.

> I have three "secondary" relationships; none of them are primary because we are in a polyfidelity closed group marriage.
>
> —Bisexual female

> I consider our group polyfidelitous, so we're allowed to do all these things with each other but not [with] someone outside of the group.
>
> —Heterosexual male

> We are a triad, three people involved exclusively with each other.
>
> —Heterosexual female

Polyfidelity allows for multiple sexual or emotional partners but maintains a certain level of commitment through exclusivity among those involved. Though this may seem contradictory, polyfidelity epitomizes the notion that commitment and fidelity can occur among multiple partners, alone or together. For example, one respondent commented that extratriadic behaviors were not allowed:

> We are in a closed triad—I guess you could call it polyfidelity—but it basically means that there are to be no encounters outside the triad. If someone does do something outside the triad, it would be considered cheating.
>
> —Bisexual female

Although some polyamorists had incorporated traditional (that is, exclusivity-centered) notions of fidelity into their multiple-partner relationships, most interviewees' experiences, comments, situations, and speculations contextualize agentic fidelity in terms of what polyamory meant to them:

> Polyamory means that I am committed to my partners by having total, honest communication. I can enjoy all the benefits of polyamory—to give others the gift of pleasure which you might not have otherwise. Monogamy creates this tension all the time between people's desires and what they are allowed to do or not do and I just see that as foolish. Polyamory lets people enjoy pleasure and bond with others in a way that is trustworthy because we are upfront about our boundaries and try to respect them.
>
> —Martin, 29, heterosexual

Therefore, fidelity in polyamory is not really about sexual or emotional exclusivity; it is rather a form of chosen commitment to open, honest communication, disclosure when desired, and determining what is considered special between different partners. Agentic fidelity involves remaining loyal to the process of establishing agreements and rules in polyamorous relationships. It also means respecting oneself and one's partners by following the rules, whatever they may be.

Polyamorists set their own stage for trustworthiness in respecting boundaries regardless of what they may entail, and a polyamorist ideology has become more pervasive in assisting individuals with this process. While I was conducting interviews with polyamorists, a pattern emerged in which many took time to provide a "poly primer" before, during, or after the interview. This involved defining key terms and phrases, such as *new relationship energy* (NRE), *total honesty, compersion,* and *veto power.* Several also described the history of polyamory, where the term had originated, and what polyamory both is and is not, offering to e-mail me links to websites, blog posts, and other reading material as necessary. Although polyamorists seem to have a highly autonomous approach to constructing their intimate lives and maintaining commitment through agentic fidelity, they also engage a specified ideology.

Polyamory challenges mononormative notions of love, sex, and intimacy by explicitly resisting sexual and emotional exclusivity, offering the most comprehensive alternative to the traditional master template of relationships. At the same time, polyamorists ultimately confirm the centrality of dual fidelity in romantic relationships by constituting themselves as its opposite in both ideology and behavior. However, by underscoring the absence of restrictions on multiple loves, polyamorists emphasize the value of emotional rather than sexual intimacy. Polyamorists negotiate the intricacies of multiple partners through formal agreements that are most often verbal and written, whereas other forms of nonmonogamy prefer "don't ask, don't tell" policies and verbal (or no) official agreements. Although rules remain central to both nonmonogamous and polyamorous relationships, there are differences in their focus and intent. Safer sex rules are a concern for all types of nonmonogamy, but polyamorous agreements focus on active communication, honesty, and disclosure in facilitating relations among multiple partners. Through a framework of constructive objectives rather than restrictive limitations, polyamorists shift the focus of rules from what partners should not do with others to what partners should do for the good of all the relationships and individuals involved.

Polyamorists are not immune to tensions between master templates and subversive narratives. Interviewees described their struggles with simultaneously preserving both autonomy and feeling special in their array of sexual, romantic, and affective partnerships. Though some resisted the notion of specialness as a construct inherent to monogamous relationship design, most interviewees and survey respondents described rules, interactions, and renegotiations that reflected efforts to preserve "something different" with each partner. And although many follow the rules of their relationships, some polyamorists do in fact break them. As they are for other nonmonogamists, the consequences of rule infractions among polyamorists are geared more toward renegotiation than toward relationship disengagement. Polyamorists also actively distinguish themselves from other nonmonogamists because of their ability and desire to engage multiple emotional or love partners. However, they assert the value and importance of emotional connectedness, emphasizing their ability to fall in love with more than one person.

When polyamorists violate the rules, agentic fidelity is further achieved through investment in renegotiation rather than through the dissolution of the relationship. The very acts of establishing and enacting the rules of polyamory serve as indicators of commitment.

Finally, although commitment evokes traditional notions of dual fidelity, polyamorists have successfully redefined fidelity in terms of multiple-partner exclusivity. Polyamorous notions of agentic fidelity include commitment to establishing rules, communication regarding boundaries and desires, and devotion to renegotiation. If polyamory effectively contributes to the deinstitutionalization of monogamy through multiple sexual *and* emotional possibilities, then the rules that characterize such relationships reflect shifts in sex, love, and romance.

ENDNOTES

1. One interviewee was heavily involved in the Sexual Freedom League and had participated in a number of studies on open marriage and polyamory in the late 1960s.

2. *Polyamory* entered the *Oxford English Dictionary* in 1992 as a noun, defined as "the fact of having simultaneous close emotional relationships with two or more other individuals, viewed as an alternative to monogamy, esp. in regard to matters of sexual fidelity; the custom or practice of engaging in multiple sexual relationships with the knowledge and consent of all partners concerned" (*OED* Online, s.v. "polyamory," accessed September 10, 2007. http://dictionary.oed.com/cgi/entry/50084 378).

3. This study's design initially fell short in recognizing such distinctions. However, once data collection began, I made a serious effort to accommodate the needs of specifically polyamorous respondents. For example, several survey questions did not allow for multiple primary partners; however, participants were able to respond as needed through open-ended questions. During in-depth interviews, particular attention was given to nuancing polyamory through interviewer questions.

4. Several researchers have explored the connection between the BDSM/kink subculture and polyamory, suggesting that the two share similar values (honesty, communication, safety; see Sheff 2005, 2006). Both BDSM practitioners and polyamorists play with breaking a number of standard forms of relation and social interaction.

5. One respondent in particular e-mailed me on several occasions to express her concern that whatever data I gathered on cheating "would never yield any measurable, generalizable results worth publishing" because the survey was "mononormative, biased and poor social science research."

CHAPTER 6

RENOVATING RELATIONAL COMMITMENT

PERSONAL FIDELITY AND FEELING SPECIAL

Romantic relationships ultimately involve nuanced fidelities that reflect ideas of sex, love, and commitment that are not necessarily predicated upon monogamy. Strict monogamy has been so culturally and institutionally emphasized that it has become the currency of sex, intimacy, and romantic love through the reinforcement (and therefore explicit acceptance) of sexual and emotional exclusivity. This book highlights fidelity as very much a part of today's romantic relationships; however, fidelity does not necessarily rely on dual exclusivity. *Contemporary fidelity*, as I call it, ranges from relationship to relationship, allows for an embrace of the master template, and simultaneously locates those who modify commitment to fit their own needs and desires.

A core component of contemporary fidelity is investigating how individuals conceptualize monogamy. Interviewees were quick to point out that monogamy means "being" with one person but failed to adequately articulate what monogamy comprises. This is primarily due to the hegemonic template of monogamy, which is not questioned or thought about because there are no socially sanctioned alternatives (Previti and Amato 2003). Further, individuals seldom explicitly agree upon monogamy when developing their relationships; for most, it is assumed, implied, and rarely verbalized.[1] Therefore, assessing what monogamy means is useful in identifying its practitioners, benefits, and limitations.

Contemporary fidelity also allows a more flexible approach to commitment through a reconsideration of what constitutes sex. Defining sex has been a neglected point in examinations of intimate relationships because it is generally assumed to be penile–vaginal intercourse. What actually constitutes sex (and therefore sexual interaction) in assessing extramarital permissiveness and behavior has relied upon a limited heterosexual definition of intercourse. For example, research indicates that oral–genital contact is not considered sex by as much as 59% of the population, and 19% do not consider penile–anal penetration to be sex (Sanders and Reinisch 1999; Risman and Schwartz 2002). The definition of sex affects reporting rates, as well as perceptions of, engagement in, and responses to extradyadic sexual contact. What constitutes sex, therefore, affects what is considered cheating.

Another characteristic of contemporary fidelity is an intentional distinction between sexual and emotional exclusivity that provides the opportunity to remain emotionally monogamous while engaging in extradyadic sexual behavior (or to remain sexually monogamous while emotionally engaging with other partners). This distinction affects what is considered cheating and also identifies a segment of monogamous relationships that participate in veiled fidelity. Rather than subscribing to covert extradyadic interactions, some have navigated the difficult terrain of sexual desire and monogamy by creating agreements or tacit understandings of permissible sexual interactions with others. Individuals who engage in veiled fidelity are often hard to identify, given that most identify as monogamous. Some even hide behind veiled fidelity, wishing to appear monogamous—and therefore socially

approved—while fulfilling their extradyadic desires in a mostly monogamous context.

Nonmonogamists are often regarded as unable to commit, disloyal,
and sexually licentious (Fletcher 2002). But nonmonogamy can (and
does) involve both commitment and fidelity, although it is operationalized through differentiations between sexual and emotional exclusivity.
This occurs in one of two main ways: (1) resisting sexual but accepting
emotional fidelity or (2) resisting both sexual and emotional fidelity.
Instead of completely discarding the master template of dual fidelity,
some distinguish between love and sex in order to preserve commitment.
The result is a form of contemporary fidelity predicated on emotional
rather than sexual exclusivity. Other nonmonogamists resist both sexual
and emotional fidelity yet still have ways of ensuring fidelity and demonstrating commitment between partners, although they do not require
exclusivity.

The structure and rules of monogamy are normed and institutionalized, thus providing social support for these relationship goals.
Strict monogamous and mostly monogamous relationships involve tacit
and most often implied rules and boundaries about exclusivity and
commitment. For many monogamists, perceptions of nonmonogamy are
conceptualized in terms of promiscuity rather than consensual, "ethical"
multiple partners. But nonmonogamy does involve establishing agreements that restrict or enable sexual and nonsexual behavior with others.
These agreements entail explicit rather than implicit rules that ultimately serve as the master template of nonmonogamous relationships,
offering the commitment, love, and specialness that dual fidelity seemingly provides. The result is a contemporary approach to intimacy that
relies not on sexual exclusivity but rather on regulations that prevent
multiple love bonds and thus ensure emotional fidelity.

Polyamory, by definition, resists dual fidelity, allowing for multiple
sexual and emotional partners. In constructing polyamory, much as
in consensual nonmonogamy, individuals establish or create agree-

ments that restrict or permit behavior with others. These rules structure nonmonogamous relationships, offering the commitment, love, and specialness that dual fidelity seemingly provides. Polyamorous relationships, although assumed to be free-for-alls, draw on such rules to enable those involved to maintain multiple sexual and emotional bonds. Much like rules in other forms of nonmonogamy, polyamorous rules center on safer sex. However, these rules tend to be less about restricting certain sexual or nonsexual behaviors and more about encouraging a polyamorous lifestyle predicated upon communication, disclosure, and renegotiation. In the negotiation, existence, governance, breaking, and renegotiation of rules in polyamorous relationships, fidelity between partners is, for some, achieved apart from sex or love.

Further, the rules themselves rather than what they govern become the defining characteristic of polyamory, demonstrating the value, importance, and worth of emotional (albeit multiple) connectedness. Rules in polyamorous relationships grant some semblance of power to all individuals involved and ultimately serve as indicators of commitment because they have been negotiated between partners. By underscoring their ability for multiple loves, polyamorists demonstrate a continued emphasis on emotion rather than sex. The result is a modified approach to intimacy that ensures fidelity not through sexual or emotional facets but through the existence of rules that mediate them.

Today's romantic relationships involve a range of fidelities based on elements of sex, love, exclusivity, and agency. Chapter 1 discussed ways that fidelity has traditionally been operationalized as sexual and emotional exclusivity through the master marriage template. For most, monogamy is synonymous with fidelity. However, as I have shown, fidelity can and often is achieved between individuals in a variety of relationships considered monogamous, nonmonogamous, or polyamorous. Previous research on romantic bonds has remained largely peripheral to sociology, and the studies that exist have approached intimate relationships and fidelity through contexts of normalization (as in literature on marriage and the family) or deviance (as in literature on cheating and swinging). Few have examined the meaning and role of fidelity outside the context of mononormative definitions of love, sex, and commitment—a lack that this research attempts to rectify.

This study's interview and survey data from monogamists, nonmonogamists, and polyamorists present a portrait of contemporary fidelities that is multidimensional, though relational concepts like love, sex, and monogamy remain influential. Analysis of the ways romantic relationships are constructed and maintained reveals that the rules of relationships and the role of renegotiation contribute to preserving commitment in four main types of fidelity. The fidelity typology is delineated in terms of whether individuals accepted or resisted sexual or emotional exclusivity, whether individual behavior aligned with ideology, and what role individual agency played in determining commitment.

There were two kinds of monogamists in this study: those who accepted and practiced both sexual and emotional exclusivity through the ideology of monogamy, and those who accepted the tenets of monogamy but behaved to the contrary. Chapter 2 focused on strict monogamists, who accepted monogamy in both ideology and behavior. Strict monogamists followed the socially normed rules of monogamy; they were in love and had sexual relations with only each other. Dual fidelity was central to strict monogamy because dual exclusivity provided commitment and security, as exemplified in strict monogamists' perceptions, definitions, and demonstrations of monogamy and love. Conceptualizations of monogamy involved inferring emotional exclusivity through sexual fidelity and also continued to be socially and institutionally ingrained through assessments of its perceived benefits and limitations.

Chapter 3 examined mostly monogamous individuals, who accepted the tenets of monogamy but sometimes behaved otherwise. Fidelity was still central to the mostly monogamous. However, I characterized it as veiled because it is an obscured form of loyalty and is often hidden behind because it resembles the master template. Veiled fidelity upholds monogamy as an ideology but challenges its expectations of sexual and emotional exclusivity through mostly covert, but sometimes consensual, extradyadic behavior. The definition of sex, as well as what was considered cheating, informed the significance of veiled fidelity. Further, the mostly monogamous preserved veiled fidelity and demonstrated loyalty by differentiating sex and love. For both strict and mostly monogamists, operationalizing monogamy, sex, and love was vital to effectively capturing their romantic relationship experiences.

Nonmonogamy took a variety of forms in this study. Chapters 4 and 5 explored the meaning and role of fidelity in nonmonogamous and polyamorous relationships, which have traditionally been perceived as unrestricted and lacking faithfulness and commitment. Fidelity remained a central concept for both nonmonogamists and polyamorists, although it was conceptualized and operationalized through rules, regulations, and an alternative ideology to dual exclusivity. Nonmonogamists employed specified fidelity to distinguish between love and sex for the sake of preserving specialness between primary partners. Polyamorists resisted both sexual and emotional exclusivity in constructing their relationships with multiple partners, although fidelity remained salient. Agentic fidelity involved the most personal agency because polyamorists chose what constituted commitment between partners.

Rules were central to all relationship types, and chapters 2 through 5 demonstrated that regulations ranged from being institutionalized to being agentically actualized. Strict monogamists typically did not negotiate the rules of their relationships because they have been socially and institutionally normed. The perceptions and experiences of monogamists clearly affected and sustained commitment in their relationships. Mostly monogamous individuals upheld the ideology of monogamy but at times violated the rules through their definitions of sex and cheating. For nonmonogamists and polyamorists, the very process of establishing agreements and rules governing sexual and nonsexual interactions with others was important. They actively structured their relationships to ensure that their needs and boundaries, as well as those of their partners, were heard and met. Nonmonogamists had rules that allowed for multiple sexual encounters but preserved emotional exclusivity. Polyamorists, however, had rules about communication and disclosure that invoked a polyamorous ideology predicated upon multiple sexual and emotional involvements. Especially for polyamorists, the process of establishing rules was at times more important than the behaviors and interactions the rules governed.

Gender and sexual orientation remained important factors in negotiating contemporary fidelity and determining patterns among the monogamous, nonmonogamous, and polyamorous. Most heterosexuals, especially women, had a greater tendency to accept and practice monogamy and therefore to embrace either dual or veiled fidelity. Heterosexual women were more inclined to subscribe to dual fidelity through strict monogamy, whereas heterosexual men were more likely to opt for veiled fidelity by being mostly monogamous. Gay men, however, were more likely to be in nonmonogamous relationships that involved specified fidelity, whereas lesbian women preferred strict monogamy (as indicated by survey results and follow-up interviews). These results are consistent with previous research on gendered and sexualized patterns of monogamy. Although bisexual women and men were more likely to engage in polyamory and nonmonogamy, some bisexuals reported their relationships as strictly monogamous. Gender and sexual orientation are perhaps the foremost predictors of which romantic relationship model one embraces (or resists) and of the extent to which contemporary fidelities are assumed, negotiated, or violated.

THE ROLE OF CHOICE AND PERSONAL FIDELITY IN ROMANTIC RELATIONSHIPS

Struening (2002) suggested that because today's relationships involve a greater emphasis on affection, emotional support, and sexual pleasure, individuals have demanded more freedom to make their own decisions about how they order their intimate lives:

> Today's marriages and partnerships, unlike marriages in the past, are based primarily on feelings of affection and love ... at the core is the belief that the individuals engaging in a love relationship must be free to define it in their own way. Decisions concerning intimate relationships should not be controlled by external expectations or social conventions. To do so would be to undermine the very possibility of true intimacy.
>
> (Struening 2002, 14)

Individuating decisions about and choices within relationships invoke agency and a sense of freedom that most socially mitigated relationships lack. In fact, even marriage is now regarded more as a choice than a legal, religious, or social necessity (Miller 2012).

This study shows patterns of choice about and within each relationship type, especially in regard to fidelity. A majority of the strictly monogamous individuals had apparently not explicitly chosen monogamy. Rather, they entered into their relationships assuming strict monogamy and expecting dual fidelity. Further, most who assumed or expected monogamy were heterosexual, which speaks to monogamy's heteronormativity. Even a majority of the mostly monogamous described assuming rather than clearly choosing monogamy, although one could argue that this explains why many engaged in veiled fidelity.

The experiences of the few who did choose monogamy highlighted several features. First, most were gay men or bisexual women and men. All gay male interviewees who were monogamous described choosing and agreeing upon monogamy with their partners. Many bisexual women and men also described the process of choosing monogamy, given that bisexuality has been commonly equated with promiscuity based on dual attraction. Second, some interviewees had previously tried nonmonogamous alternatives, such as open relationships or threesomes, and for various reasons had decided they wanted to be monogamous. A few described a more dimensional reasoning for monogamy—choosing it "for *this* relationship I'm in," therefore based on the current partner, or choosing it "right *now* in this relationship," based on a periodic approach to monogamy that may later fluctuate. Some reported that their experiences with nonmonogamy had yielded a process of self-reflection that included a "not for me" realization, and these study participants had since actively chosen monogamy.

And though the discourse of choice seemed more elaborate in nonmonogamous relationships, a question arises: Was there really more choice? Nonmonogamists and polyamorists created rules and agreements about partners and behaviors that resisted the dominant paradigm, yet they continued to incorporate fidelity through emotional exclusivity, specialness between certain partners, and adherence to a polyamorous ideology. Although those in nonmonogamous and polyamorous relationships subverted the master template by deciding what constitutes commitment, they did so within informed relationship structures (though these were resistant of mononormativity).

The four main types of fidelity in monogamous, nonmonogamous, and polyamorous relationships illustrate that loyalty and commitment are more multidimensional than the traditional master template indicates. The characteristics of contemporary fidelity involve distinctions between love and sex, between sexual and emotional exclusivity, and between ideology and behavior—but the role of personal choice was a recurring theme in various contexts of negotiating relationships and relational concepts. For example, agentic fidelity certainly involved a more individualistic approach.

A central component of the rules of nonmonogamy and polyamory was the ability to be aware of and articulate one's own sexual and emotional needs, desires, and boundaries in constructing the rules (and subsequently following them). Such self-knowledge can be difficult to achieve, especially given that sexual and emotional exclusivity have become deeply culturally and institutionally entrenched. Recognizing and articulating one's own needs while simultaneously conveying them to multiple partners requires a self-involvement and individual commitment that emerged in the data and that warrants future research. I call this *personal fidelity* because the responsibility to acknowledge, convey, and meet one's needs ultimately falls on the individual.

However, personal fidelity may not be completely individualistic and may instead originate vis-à-vis the often established agreements and rules about sexual and emotional exclusivities between partners. Burke and Stets (1999) alluded to this notion as trust and commitment through self-verification. It becomes a less explicitly designated dimension of protecting one's partner and preserving specialness, and it serves as an additional reflection of commitment to the relationship(s). Personal fidelity may become the hallmark of how individuals maneuver through their intimate relationships, and authenticity is paramount in adhering to it. Though personal fidelity is ultimately informed by social norms and institutions, the master marriage template, and differentiating sex and love to a certain degree, it is also largely based on an individual's sexual and emotional self-awareness, accountability, and perceived responsibility to one's partner(s).

The rules of personal fidelity are essentially decided by the individual without an explicit agreement or discussion involving someone else. However, self-imposed rules still invoke the preservation of specialness, in some cases ensure emotional exclusivity, and are often aligned with rules that have already, in some way, been explicitly negotiated. Further, even though the rules of monogamy, nonmonogamy, and polyamory are ultimately followed or broken through individual choice, there are institutional and social consequences for those who violate the rules of their relationship(s). When the rules of one's own personal fidelity are violated, accountability and liability rest with the individual. Loyalty is therefore self-generated, self-preserved, self-actualized, and self-enforced regardless of one's relationship structure or the partner(s) involved.

The empirical materials presented coalesce to offer a range of fidelities that characterize contemporary intimate relationships. However, although monogamists, nonmonogamists, and polyamorists in this study varied in terms of defining love and sex, differentiating between sexual and emotional exclusivity, and engaging individual agency, there was one constant in each and every relationship type: the desire to be and feel special. Why is specialness so important? Why must individuals feel special to their partner(s) and ensure that their partner(s) also feel special?

Cooley (1902) suggested that a person's self and therefore identity grow out of one's interpersonal interactions with and perceptions of others. Although it may seem dated, this self-concept principle may offer a simple yet ideal explanation as to why fidelity retains such importance, albeit in varied forms. Loyalty validates a person's existence not only to other people and to society but also, ultimately, to oneself. Recognition by others, especially in the form of prioritization, gives people meaning in their lives, helps them achieve self-realization and self-fulfillment, and contributes to their developing a sense of authenticity (Weeks 2011).

Exclusivity is an understandable conduit for allegiance to another and devotion to the other's desires. Sharing a unique connection, behavior, or experience with someone distinguishes and ultimately prioritizes that particular bond, setting it apart from others and thus affirming one's worthiness and relevance as an individual. The participants in this study demonstrate that loyalty, commitment, and faithfulness matter both individually and socially; fidelity, in its organic, authentic, tailored, disparate forms, is the most relevant template for contemporary intimacies. With dual fidelity, feeling special is achieved among strict monogamists through sexual and emotional exclusivity. Veiled fidelity preserves specialness for the mostly monogamous, and nonmonogamists employ specified fidelity in order to ensure specialness between partners. Polyamorists engage agentic fidelity in retaining specialness between multiple emotional and sexual partners. And those, regardless of relationship type, who enact personal fidelity individuate feeling special and underscore the importance of one's own boundaries, desires, and worth. Ultimately, feeling special matters because it reinforces an individual's significance to oneself and to others. Perhaps this is why intimate relationships, in their nuanced and varied forms, retain such importance and continue to be sought after and revered; they are especially momentous, influential, and meaningful on both an individual and a societal level.

ENDNOTES

1. Although marriage vows can and do serve as a formal agreement, rarely do intentional agreements about sexual and emotional exclusivity take place in monogamous relationships.

BIBLIOGRAPHY

Adam, Barry. 2006. "Relationship Innovation in Male Couples." *Sexualities* 9 (1): 5–26.

Anapol, Debora M. 1997. *Polyamory: The New Love Without Limits; Secrets of Sustainable Intimate Relationships*. San Rafael, CA: IntiNet Resource Center.

Atwater, Lynn. 1979. "Women and Marriage: Adding an Extramarital Role." In *Social Interaction*, edited by Howard Robboy, Sidney Greenblat, and Candace Clark, 510–520. New York: St. Martin's Press.

———. 1982. *The Extramarital Connection: Sex, Intimacy, and Identity*. New York: Irvington.

Ault, Amber. 1996. "Ambiguous Identity in an Unambiguous Sex/Gender Structure: The Case of Bisexual Women." *Sociological Quarterly* 37 (3): 449–463.

Barash, David P., and Judith Lipton. 2001. *The Myth of Monogamy: Fidelity and Infidelity in Animals and People*. New York: W. H. Freeman.

Barker, Meg. 2005. "This is My Partner, and This is My ... Partner's Partner: Constructing a Polyamorous Identify in a Monogamous World." *Journal of Constructivist Psychology* 18: 75–88.

Barker, Meg, and Darren Langdridge, eds. 2009. *Understanding Non-monogamies*. London: Routledge.

Bergstrand, Curtis R., and Jennifer Blevins Sinski. 2010. *Swinging in America: Love, Sex, and Marriage in the 21st Century*. Santa Barbara, CA: Praeger.

Berscheid, E., and L. A. Peplau. 1983. "The Emerging Science of Relationships." In *Close Relationships*, edited by H. Kelley et al., 1–19. New York: W. H. Freeman.

Blinn-Pike, Lynn. 1999. "Why Abstinent Adolescents Report They Have Not Had Sex: Understanding Sexually Resilient Youth." *Family Relations* 48 (3): 295–301.

Blow, Adrian J., and Kelley Hartnett. 2005a. "Infidelity in Committed Relationships I: A Methodological Review." *Journal of Marital and Family Therapy* 31 (2): 183–216.

———. 2005b. "Infidelity in Committed Relationships II: A Substantive Review." *Journal of Marital and Family Therapy* 31 (2): 217–233.

Blumstein, Phil, and Pepper Schwartz. 1983. *American Couples.* New York: Morrow.

Bonello, Kristoff, and Malcolm C. Cross. 2009. "Gay Monogamy: I Love You But I Can't Have Sex with Only You." *Journal of Homosexuality* 57: 117–139.

Brecher, Edward. 1969. *The Sex Researchers.* Boston: Little, Brown & Co.

Brown, Susan. 2005. "How Cohabitation is Reshaping American Families." *Contexts* 4: 33–37.

Budgeon, Shelley. 2008. "Couple Culture and the Production of Singleness." *Sexualities* 11: 301–325.

Burke, Peter, and Jan Stets. 1999. "Trust and Commitment Through Self-Verification." *Social Psychology Quarterly* 62: 347–366.

Buss, D., R. Larsen, D. Westen, and J. Semmelroth. 1992. "Sex Differences in Jealousy: Evolution, Physiology, and Psychology." *Psychological Social Science* 3: 251–255.

Buunk, Bram. 1980. "Extramarital Sex in the Netherlands." *Alternative Lifestyles* 3: 11–39.

———. 1982. "Strategies of Jealousy: Styles of Coping with Extramarital Involvement of the Spouse." *Family Relations* 31 (1): 13–18.

Cancian, Francesca M. 1987. *Love in America: Gender and Self-Development.* New York: Cambridge University Press.

Chambers, David L. 2001. "What If? The Legal Consequences of Marriage and the Legal Needs of Lesbian and Gay Male Couples." In *Queer Families, Queer Politics: Challenging Culture and the State*, edited by

Mary Bernstein and Renate Reimann, 306–337. New York: Columbia University Press.

Charles, M. 2002. "Monogamy and its Discontents: On Winning the Oedipal War." *American Journal of Psychoanalysis* 62 (2): 119–143.

Charmaz, Kathy. 2001. "Qualitative Interviewing and Grounded Theory Analysis." In *Handbook of Interview Research: Context and Method*, edited by James Gubrium and Jaber Holstein, 675–694. Thousand Oaks, CA: Sage.

Cherlin, Andrew. 1999. *Public and Private Families.* Boston: McGraw-Hill.

———. 2002. *Public and Private Lives: An Introduction.* New York: McGraw-Hill.

Cloud, J. 1999. "Henry & Mary & Janet & ... Is Your Marriage a Little Dull? The "Polyamorists" Say There's Another Way." *Time* 154 (20).

Cole, Charles, and Graham Spanier. 1974. "Comarital Mate-Sharing and Family Stability." *Journal of Sex Research* 10: 21–31.

Coleman, Eli. 1985. "Bisexual Women in Marriages." *Journal of Homosexuality*, 11 (1–2): 87–99.

Coltrane, Scott, and Randall Collins. 2001. *Sociology of Marriage and the Family: Gender, Love, and Property.* 5th ed. Belmont, CA: Wadsworth.

Constantine, L. L., J. M. Constantine, and S. K. Edelman. 1985. "Counseling Implications of Comarital and Multilateral Relations." *Family Coordinator* 21 (3): 267–273.

Cook, Elaine. 2005. "Commitment in Polyamorous Relationships." Unpublished master's thesis. Available at www.aphroweb.net.

Cooley, Charles H. 1902. *Human Nature and the Social Order.* New York: Scribner's.

Davidson, Joy. 2002. "Working with Polyamorous Clients in the Clinical Setting." *Electronic Journal of Human Sexuality* 5, http://www.ejhs.org/volume5/polyoutline.html.

Davis, D., and Smith, T. 1991. *General Social Surveys, 1972–1991.* Chicago: National Opinion Research Center, University of Chicago.

DeLamater, John. 1987. "Gender Differences in Sexual Scenarios." In *Females, Males, and Sexuality: Theories and Research*, edited by K. Kelley, 127–139. Albany, NY: SUNY Press.

Denfeld, Duane. 1974. "Dropouts from Swinging." *Family Coordinator* 23 (1): 45–49.

DeStento, D., M. Bartlee, J. Braverman, and P. Salovey. 2002. "Sex Differences in Jealousy: Evolutionary Mechanism or Artifact of Measurement? *Journal of Personality and Social Psychology* 83: 1103–1116.

Dijkstra, P., H. Groothof, G. Poel, T. Laverman, M. Schrier, and B. Buunk. (2001). "Sex Differences in the Events that Elicit Jealousy among Homosexuals." *Personal Relationships* 8: 41–54.

Dixon, Joan K. 1985. "Sexuality and Relationship Changes in Married Females Following the Commencement of Bisexual Activity." *Journal of Homosexuality* 11 (1/2): 115–133.

Easton, Dossie, and Catherine A. Liszt. 1997. *The Ethical Slut: A Guide To Infinite Sexual Possibilities.* San Francisco, CA: Greenery Press.

Emens, E. F. 2004. "Monogamy's Law: Compulsory Monogamy and Polyamorous Existence." *NYU Review of Law and Social Change* 29: 277–376.

Evans, Mary. 1993. *Love: An Unromantic Discussion.* Malden, MA: Blackwell.

Ferrer, Jorge N. 2008. "Beyond Monogamy and Polyamory: A New Vision of Intimate Relationships for the Twenty-First Century." *ReVision* 30 (1): 53–58.

Finn, Mark, and Helen Malson. 2008. "Speaking of Home Truth: (Re)productions of Dyadic-Containment in Non-monogamous Relationships." *British Journal of Social Psychology* 47: 519–533.

Fisher, Helen E. 1992. *Anatomy of Love: The Natural History of Monogamy, Adultery, and Divorce.* New York: W. W. Norton.

Fletcher, Garth. 2002. *The New Science of Intimate Relationships.* Oxford: Blackwell.

Frank, David John, Tara Hardinge, and Kassia Wosick-Correa. 2009. "The Global Dimensions of Rape-Law Reform: A Cross-National Study of Policy Outcomes." *American Sociological Review* 74 (2): 272–290.

Giddens, Anthony. 1992. *The Transformation of Intimacy: Sexuality, Love and Eroticism in Modern Societies.* Cambridge: Polity.

Gilmartin, B. G. 1977. "Swinging: Who Gets Involved and How?" In *Marriage and Alternatives: Exploring Intimate Relationships*, edited by R. W. Libby and R. N. Whitehurst, 161–185. Glenview, IL: Scott Foresman & Co.

Glaser, Barney G., and Anselm L. Strauss, 1967. *The Discovery of Grounded Theory: Strategies for Qualitative Research.* Chicago: Aldine.

Goffman, Erving. 1963. *Stigma.* Englewood Cliffs, NJ: Prentice-Hall.

Gotta, Gabrielle, Robert-Jay Green, Esther Rothblum, Sondra Solomon, Kimberly Balsam, and Pepper Schwartz. 2011. "Heterosexual, Lesbian, and Gay Male Relationships: A Comparison of Couples in 1975 and 2000." *Family Process* 50 (3): 53–376.

Gramsci, Antonio. 1971. *Selections from Prison Notebooks.* London: New Left Books.

Greeley, A. M. 1991. *Faithful Attraction: Discovering Intimacy, Love, and Fidelity in American Marriage.* New York: Doherty.

Green, Adam. 2006. "Until Death Do Us Part? The Impact of Differential Access to Marriage on a Sample of Urban Men." *Sociological Perspectives* 49 (2): 163–189.

Haeberle, Erwin, and Rolf Gindorf, eds. 1998. *Bisexualities: The Ideology and Practice of Sexual Contact with Both Men and Women.* New York: Continuum.

Hafner, Julian. 1993. *The End of Marriage: Why Monogamy Isn't Working.* London: Century.

Halberstam, Judith. 1998. *Female Masculinity.* Durham, NC: Duke University Press.

Halpern, Ellen, 1999. "If Love is So Wonderful, What's So Scary About More? *Journal of Lesbian Studies* 3 (1–2): 157–164.

Harry, Joseph. 1984. *Gay Couples.* New York: Praeger.

Hatfield, Elaine, and Richard L. Rapson. 2005. *Love and Sex: Cross-Cultural Perspectives.* New York: University Press of America.

Heckathorn, Douglas. 1997. "Respondent-Driven Sampling: A New Approach to the Study of Hidden Populations." *Social Problems* 44: 174–199.

Heinlein, Kriss A., and Rozz M. Heinlein. 2004. *The Sex and Love Handbook.* Do Things Records and Publishing.

Hendrick, Susan S. 2004. *Understanding Close Relationships.* Boston: Allyn & Bacon.

Henshel, A. 1973. "Swinging: A Study of Decision-Making in Marriage." *American Journal of Sociology* 78 (1): 975–981.

Jackson, S., and S. Scott. 2004. "The Personal *Is* Still Political: Heterosexuality, Feminism, and Monogamy. *Feminism & Psychology* 14 (1): 151–157.

Jenks, R. J. 1998. Swinging: A Review of the Literature. *Archives of Sexual Behavior* 27 (5): 507–521.

Josephs, Lawrence, and Jessica Shimberg. 2010. "The Dynamics of Sexual Fidelity: Personal Style as a Reproductive Strategy." *Psychoanalytic Psychology* 27 (3): 273–295.

Josephson, J. 2005. "Citizenship, Same-Sex Marriage, and Feminist Critiques of Marriage." *Perspectives on Politics* 3 (2): 269–284.

Kanazawa, Satoshi, and Mary Still. 1999. "Why Monogamy?" *Social Forces* 78 (1): 25–50.

Kanter, Rosabeth M. 1968. "Commitment and Social Organization: A Study of Commitment Mechanisms in Utopian Communities." *American Sociological Review* 33 (4) 499–517.

Keener, Matt C. 2004. "A Phenomenology of Polyamorous Persons." Master's thesis, University of Utah.

Kilbride, Philip. 1994. *Plural Marriage for Our Times: A Reinvented Option?* Westport, CT: Bergin & Garvey.

Kinsey, Alfred C., Wardell Pomeroy, and Clyde Martin. 1948. *Sexual Behavior in the Human Male*. Philadelphia, PA: Saunders.

Kinsey, Alfred C., Wardell Pomeroy, Clyde Martin, and Paul Gebhard. 1953. *Sexual Behavior in the Human Female*. Philadelphia, PA: Saunders.

Klein, Fritz. 1978. *The Bisexual Option*. New York: Arbor House.

Klesse, Christian. 2005. "Bisexual Women, Non-monogamy, and Differentialist Anti-promiscuity Discourses." *Sexualities* 8 (4): 445–464.

Klesse, Christian. 2006. "Polyamory and its 'Others': Contesting the Terms of Non-monogamy." *Sexualities* 9 (5): 565–583.

Klinger, E. 1977. *Meaning and Void: Inner Experience and the Incentives in People's Lives*. Minneapolis: University of Minnesota Press.

Knapp, Jacquelyn. 1976. "An Exploratory Study of Seventeen Sexually Open Marriages." *Journal of Sex Research* 12 (3): 206–219.

Knapp, Jacquelyn, and R. Whitehurst. 1977. "Sexually Open Marriage and Relationships: Issues and Prospects." In *Marriage and Alternatives: Exploring Intimate Relationships*, edited by R. W. Libby and R. N. Whitehurst, 147–160. Glenview, IL: Scott Foresman & Co.

Kuhle, Barry X., Kerrie D. Smedley, and David P. Schmitt. 2009. "Sex Differences in the Motivation and Mitigation of Jealousy-Induced Interrogations." *Personality and Individual Differences* 46: 499–502.

Kurdek, L. A., and L. A. Schmitt. 1986. "Relationship Quality of Gay Men in Closed or Open Relationships. *Journal of Homosexuality* 12 (2): 85–99.

Labriola, Kathy. 1999. "Models of Open Relationships." *Journal of Lesbian Studies* 3 (1/2): 217–225.

LaSala, M. C. 2004. "Extradyadic Sex and Gay Male Couples: Comparing Monogamous and Nonmonogamous Relationships." *Families in Society: The Journal of Contemporary Social Services* 85 (3): 405–412.

Laumann, Edward, John Gagnon, Robert Michael, and Stuart Michaels. 1994. *The Social Organization of Sexuality: Sexual Practices in the United States*. Chicago: University of Chicago Press.

Lawson, Annette. 1988. *Adultery: An Analysis of Love and Betrayal.* New York: Basic Books.

Lehr, V. 1999. *Queer Family Values: Debunking the Myth of the Nuclear Family.* Philadelphia, PA: Temple University Press.

Lever, Janet, David E. Kanouse, William H. Rogers, Sally Carson, and Rosanna Hertz. 1992. "Behavior Patterns and Sexual Identity of Bisexual Males." *Journal of Sex Research* 29 (2): 141–167.

Lever, John. 1994. "Sexual Revelations." *Advocate*, August 23, 17–24.

Macklin, Eleanor. 1980. "Nontraditional Family Forms: A Decade of Research." *Journal of Marriage and the Family* 42 (4): 905–922.

Margolin, L. 1989. "Gender and the Prerogatives of Dating and Marriage: An Experimental Assessment of a Sample of College Students." *Sex Roles* 20: 91–102.

Matik, Wendy O. 2002. *Redefining Our Relationships: Guidelines For Responsible Open Relationships.* Oakland, CA: Defiant Times Press.

Mazur, Ronald. 1973. *The New Intimacy: Open-Ended Marriage and Alternative Lifestyles.* Boston: Beacon Press.

McLean, Kirsten. 2004. "Negotiating (Non)Monogamy: Bisexuality and Intimate Relationships." Journal of Bisexuality 4 (1–2): 83–97.

Michaels, Stuart, and Alain Giami. 1999. "Review: Sexual Acts and Sexual Relationships: Asking About Sex in Surveys." *Public Opinion Quarterly* 63 (3): 401–420.

Mileham, Beatriz Lia Avila. 2007. "Online Infidelity in Internet Chat Rooms: An Ethnographic Exploration." *Computers in Human Behavior* 23: 11–31.

Miller, Rowland S. 2012. *Intimate Relationships.* New York: McGraw-Hill.

Millner, Vaughn S. 2008. "Internet Infidelity: A Case of Intimacy with Detachment." *Family Journal* 16(1): 78–82.

Mint, Pepper. 2004a. "The Power Dynamics of Cheating: Effects on Polyamory and Bisexuality." *Journal of Bisexuality* 4(3/4): 56–76.

Mint, Pepper. 2004b. "Border Wars: Swinging and Polyamory." Paper presented at Building Bridges IV Conference, Herndon, VA, October 16.

Munson, Marcia, and Judith P. Stelboum, eds. 1999. *The Lesbian Polyamory Reader: Open Relationships, Nonmonogamy, and Casual Sex.* New York: Harrington Park.

Murstein, B. I., D. Case, and S. P. Gunn. 1985. "Personality Correlates of Ex-Swingers." *Lifestyles* 8 (1): 21–35.

Noel, Melita J. 2006. "Progressive Polyamory: Considering Issues of Diversity." *Sexualities* 6: 602–620.

O'Neill, Nena, and O'Neill, George. 1972. *Open Marriage: A New Lifestyle for Couples.* New York: Evans.

Overall, Christine. 1998. "Monogamy, Nonmonogamy, and Identity." *Hypatia: A Journal of Feminist Philosophy* 13 (4): 1–17.

Pallotta-Chiarolli, M., and S. Lubowitz. 2003. "Outside Belonging": Multi-Sexual Relationships as Border Existence. *Journal of Bisexuality* 3 (1): 53–85.

Paulson, Chich, and Rebecca Markle Paulson. 1970. *Swinging: The Minimizing of Jealousy.* Philadelphia, PA: Mimeo.

Pawlicki, Paul, and Paul Larson. 2011. "The Dynamics and Conceptualizations of Non-exclusive Relationships in Gay Male Couples." *Sexual and Relationship Therapy* 26 (1): 48–60.

Peabody, S. A. 1982. "Alternative Lifestyles to Monogamous Marriage: Variants of Normal Behavior in Psychotherapy Clients." *Family Relations* 31: 425–434.

Peplau, Letitia Anne, and Adam W. Fingerhut. 2007. "The Close Relationships of Lesbians and Gay Men." *Annual Review of Psychology* 58: 405–424.

Pfeiffer, S., and P. Wong. 1989. "Multidimensional Jealousy." *Journal of Social and Personal Relationships* 6: 181–196.

Pieper, Marianne, and Robin Bauer. 2005. "Call for Papers: International Conference on Polyamory and Mono-normativity. Research Centre for Feminist, Gender & Queer Studies." University of Hamburg, Germany, November 5–6.

Previti, Denise, and Paul R Amato. 2003. "Why Stay Married? Rewards, Barriers, and Marital Stability." *Journal of Marriage and Family* 65 (3): 561–573.

Quinn, Naomi. 1982. "'Commitment' in American Marriage: A Cultural Analysis." *American Ethnologist* 9 (4): 775–798.

Ramey, James W. 1972. "Emerging Patterns of Innovative Behavior in Marriage." *Family Coordinator* 21 (4): 435–456.

———. 1975. "Intimate Groups and Networks: Frequent Consequences of Sexually Open Marriage." *Family Coordinator* 24 (4): 515–530.

Ramirez, Oscar Modesto, and Jac Brown. 2010. "Attachment Style, Rules Regarding Sex, and Couple Satisfaction: A Study of Gay Male Couples." *Australian and New Zealand Journal of Family Therapy* 31 (2): 202–213.

Ravenscroft, Anthony. 2004. *Polyamory: Roadmaps for the Clueless and Hopeful.* Santa Fe, NM: Fenris Brothers.

Reibstein, Janet, and Martin Richards. 1992. *Sexual Arrangements: Marriage and Affairs.* London: Heinemann.

Reinisch, J. M., S. A. Sanders, and M. Siemba-Davis. 1988. "The Study of Sexual Behavior in Relation to the Transmission of Human Immunodeficiency Virus: Caveats and Recommendations." *American Psychologist* 43 (1): 921–927.

Reiss, Ira L., Ronald E. Anderson, and G. C. Sponaugle. 1980. "A Multivariate Model of the Determinants of Extramarital Sexual Permissiveness." *Journal of Marriage and the Family* 42(2): 395–411.

Rich, Adrienne. 1994. "Compulsory Heterosexuality and Lesbian Existence." *Blood, Bread, and Poetry.* New York: Norton.

Ringer, R. Jeffrey. 2001. "Constituting Nonmonogamies." In *Queer Families, Queer Politics: Challenging Culture and the State*, edited by Mary Bernstein and Renate Reimann, 137–151. New York: Columbia University Press.

Risman, Barbara, and Pepper Schwartz. 2002. "After the Sexual Revolution: Gender Politics in Teen Dating." *Contexts* 1 (Spring): 16–24.

Rosenblatt, P. C. 1977. "Needed Research on Commitment in Marriage." In *Close Relationships: A Sourcebook*, edited by Clyde Hendrick and Susan S. Hendrick, 47–57. Thousand Oaks, CA: Sage.

Rubin, A. M., and J. R. Adams. 1986. "Outcomes of Sexually Open Marriages." *Journal of Sex Research,* 22 (3): 311–319.

Rubin, R. H. 2001. "Alternative Lifestyles Revisited, or Whatever Happened to Swingers, Group Marriages, and Communes?" *Journal of Family Issues* 22 (6): 711–726.

Rusbult, C. D., M. Kumashiro, E. J. Finkel, and T. Wildschut. 2002. "The War of the Roses: An Interdependence Analysis of Betrayal and Forgiveness." In *Understanding Marriage: Developments in the Study of Couple Interactions*, edited by P. Noler and J. A. Feeney, 521–281. New York, NY: Cambridge University Press.

Rust, Paula C. 1996. "Monogamy and Polyamory: Relationship Issues for Bisexuals." In *Bisexuality: The Psychology and Politics of and Invisible Minority*, edited by Beth Firestein, 127–148. Thousand Oaks, CA: Sage.

———. 2000. "Bisexuality: A Contemporary Paradox for Women." *Journal of Social Issues* 56 (2): 205–221.

Ryalls, K., and D. R. Foster. 1976. "Open Marriage: A Question of Ego Development and Marriage Counseling?" *Family Coordinator* 25 (3): 297–302.

Sanders, Stephanie A., and June Machover Reinish. 1999. "Would You Say You 'Had Sex' If…?" *Journal of the American Medical Association* 281 (January): 275–277.

Schmookler, Terra, and Krisanne Bursik. 2007. "The Value of Monogamy in Emerging Adulthood: A Gendered Perspective." *Journal of Social and Personal Relationships* 24 (6): 819–835.

Schwandt, T. A. 2000. "Three Epistemological Stances for Qualitative Inquiry: Interpretivism, Hermeneutics, and Social Constructionism."

In *Handbook of Qualitative Research*, edited by N. K. Denzin and Y. S. Lincoln, 199–213. Thousand Oaks, CA: Sage.

Shannon, Deric, and Abbey Willis. 2010. "Theoretical Polyamory: Some Thoughts on Loving, Thinking, and Queering Anarchism." *Sexualities* 13 (4): 433–443.

Sheff, Elisabeth. 2005. "Polyamorous Women, Sexual Subjectivity, and Power." *Journal of Contemporary Ethnography* 34 (3): 251–283.

———. 2006. "The Reluctant Polyamorist: Auto-ethnographic Research in a Sexualized Setting." In *Sex Matters: The Sexuality and Society Reader*, edited by M. Stombler et al., 111–118. New York: Allyn & Bacon.

———. 2011. "Polyamorous Families, Same-Sex Marriage, and the Slippery Slope." *Journal of Contemporary Ethnography* 40 (5): 487–520.

Shumway, David R. 2003. *Modern Love: Romance, Intimacy, and the Marriage Crisis.* New York: New York University Press.

Skeggs, Beverly. 2001. "Feminist Ethnography." In *Handbook of Ethnography*, edited by Paul Atkinson et al., 426–443. London: Sage.

Smith, James, and Lynn G. Smith. 1970. "Co-marital Sex and the Sexual Freedom Movement." *Journal of Sex Research* 6 (May): 131–142.

———. 1974. *Beyond Monogamy: Recent Studies of Sexual Alternatives in Marriage.* Baltimore: Johns Hopkins University Press.

Spanier, G. B., and R. L. Margolis. 1983. "Marital Separation and Extramarital Sexual Behavior." *Journal of Sex Research* 19: 23–48.

Sprey, Jetse. 1972. "Family Power Structure: A Critical Comment." *Journal of Marriage and the Family* 34 (2): 235–238.

Strassberg, Maura. 2003. "The Challenge of Post-modern Polygamy: Considering Polyamory." *Capital University Law Review* 31 (3): 439–563.

Strauss, A., and Corbin, J. 1998. *Basics of Qualitative Research.* Thousand Oaks, CA: Sage.

Struening, Karen. 2002. *New Family Values.* Lanham, MD: Rowman & Littlefield.

Swidler, Ann. 2001. *Talk of Love: How Culture Matters.* Chicago: University of Chicago Press.

Symonds, Carolyn. 1970. "The Utopian Aspects of Sexual Mate Swapping." SSSP paper referenced in Macklin, Eleanor. 1980. "Nontraditional Family Forms: A Decade of Research." *Journal of Marriage and the Family* 42 (4): 905–922.

Thompson, Anthony Peter. 1983. "Extramarital Sex: A Review of the Research Literature." *Journal of Sex Research* 19: 1–22.

———. 1984. "Emotional and Sexual Components of Extramarital Relations." *Journal of Marriage and the Family* 46 (1): 35–42.

Treas, Judith, and Dierdre. 2000. "Sexual Infidelity among Married and Cohabitating Americans." *Journal of Marriage and the Family* 62 (1): 48–60.

Varni, Charles. 1972. "An Exploratory Study of Spouse Swapping." *Pacific Sociological Review* 15 (October): 507–522.

Wade, T. Joel., Gretchen Auer, and Tanya M. Roth. 2009. "What is Love: Further Investigation of Love Acts." *Journal of Social, Evolutionary, and Cultural Psychology* 3 (4): 290–304.

Warner, Michael. 1999. *The Trouble with Normal: Sex, Politics, and the Ethics of Queer Life.* New York: Free Press.

Watters, J. K., and P. Biernacki. 1989. "Targeted Sampling: Options for the Study of Hidden Populations." *Social Problems* 36 (4): 416–430.

Weeks, Jeffrey. 2011. *The Languages of Sexuality.* London: Routledge.

Weinberg, Martin, Collin Williams, and Douglas Prior. 1994. *Dual Attraction: Understanding Bisexuality.* New York: Oxford University Press.

Weinberg, Martin, Rochelle Swensson, and Sue Hammersmith. 1983. "Sexual Autonomy and the Status of Women: Models of Female Sexuality in the U.S. Sex Manuals from 1950–1980." *Social Problems* 30: 197–218.

Weis, David L., and Michael Slosnerick. 1981. "Attitudes toward Sexual and Nonsexual Extramarital Involvements among a Sample of College Students." *Journal of Marriage and the Family* 43 (2): 349–358.

Weitzman, Geri. 2006. "Therapy with Clients Who Are Bisexual and Polyamorous." *Journal of Bisexuality* 6 (1–2): 137–164.

Wosick-Correa, Kassia R. 2006. "Identity and Community: The Social Construction of Bisexuality in Women." In *Sex Matters: The Sexuality and Society Reader*, edited by Mindy Stombler et al., 42–52. Boston: Allyn & Bacon.

Zell, Morning Glory. 1990. "A Bouquet of Lovers: Strategies for Responsible Open Relationships." *Green Egg Magazine* 89 (Electronic edition), http://original.caw.org/articles/bouquet.html.

Ziskin, J., and M. Ziskin. 1973. *The Extra-marital Sex Contract.* Los Angeles: Nash.

———. 1975. "Co-marital Sex Agreements: An Emerging Issue in Sexual Counseling. *Counseling Psychologist* 5 (1): 81–84.

INDEX

ABOUT THE AUTHOR

Kassia R. Wosick is an assistant professor of sociology at New Mexico State University. She holds a PhD and an MA from the University of California, Irvine, and a BA from the University of Wisconsin, Eau Claire. Dr. Wosick has published in several journals such as *American Sociological Review*, *Journal of Sex Research*, and *Psychology and Sexuality*.

CPSIA information can be obtained at www.ICGtesting.com
Printed in the USA
BVOW08*1840130616

451864BV00002B/3/P